# ADVANCE PRAISE

"Rarely I meet authors that can connect spiritually with their audience. Most of them nourish my intellect, but *Cuts of a Diamond* touched my soul. I want more..."

**Alina Apostol,** Psychologist

"Sandra Bicknell writes her incredible life story from her heart, and what a heart this author has—hers is filled with nothing but love and compassion, especially for those who have hurt her throughout the half-century that encompasses her life. Her honest outlook, self-examination and positive approach are examples to follow, her insight a beacon of light."

**Anna Ruth Henriques,** Painter, Jewelry Designer and Author of *The Book Of Mechtilde*

"Sandra Rodriguez Bicknell's memoir is wonderful insight on life and love where she manages to perfectly capture the simplicity yet complexity of LOVE. It deals with relationships, joy, heartbreak, forgiveness and the discovery of self."

**Kerry-Ann Clarke,** Founder of Kerry manwomanhome

# CUTS OF A
# DIAMOND

# CUTS OF A
# DIAMOND

*Turn even your most heartbreaking experience
into a thing of beauty.*

SANDRA RODRIGUEZ BICKNELL

NEW YORK

LONDON • NASHVILLE • MELBOURNE • VANCOUVER

# Cuts of a Diamond

*Turn even your most heartbreaking experience into a thing of beauty.*

© 2019 Sandra Rodriguez Bicknell

Published in New York, New York, by Morgan James Publishing. Morgan James is a trademark of Morgan James, LLC. www.MorganJamesPublishing.com

ISBN 978-1-64279-206-5 paperback
ISBN 978-1-64279-207-2 eBook
Library of Congress Control Number: 2018952131

**Cover Design by:**
Omar Martin, Passion Fruit Jamaica

**Interior Design by:**
Megan Whitney Dillon
Creative Ninja Designs
megan@creativeninjadesigns.com

In an effort to support local communities, raise awareness and funds, Morgan James Publishing donates a percentage of all book sales for the life of each book to Habitat for Humanity Peninsula and Greater Williamsburg.

Get involved today! Visit
www.MorganJamesBuilds.com

Adrian and Leah, who have been my strength and motivation to always, do "Me."

And to all my loves.

*There are all kinds of love in this world but never the same love twice.*

F. SCOTT FITZGERALD

# CONTENT

# FOREWORD

I first met Sandra Bicknell over 20 years ago when she came to see me as a client at my complementary wellness center (Healing Hands) in Jamaica, where we were both living at the time.

Sandra was going through the effects of her marriage breaking up. Often emotional pain will show up as physical pain, especially if we do not have an outlet to honor it and transmute it. We made an immediate connection back then which has stood the test of time.

Our life paths crossed again in 2016 when she contacted me regarding life coaching. I was now living in the USA and had transitioned to using my healing skills as a personal and business success coach, helping my clients to make the emotional and mental shifts that are necessary to create joyful and sustainable success.

Sandra was ready to break the repetitive patterns of putting others happiness above her own. She was ready to love herself as fiercely as she loved others. She wanted to be able to unapologetically accept herself and be completely comfortable in her own skin. To really know, on the deepest level of herself, that she was worthy and deserving of love without needing to prove it or have it validated by the outside world.

She also wanted to align powerfully with her greater life purpose and get the clarity that would allow her to freely step into what her soul was calling her to next. This was the journey that we began with 1:1 coaching and completed when she attended my Weekend Soul Retreat in 2017.

It as been my honor to be one of Sandra's guides on her journey. I am more than thrilled to see where she has landed.

Sandra's down-to-earth, personable, funny and engaging personality comes through in this easy to read memoir. As you read her story, it is my hope that as you are entertained and engaged by retelling of her life's adventures, you will see what is possible for you too. That you are encouraged, inspired and motivated to embark upon, or continue, your own journey of self empowerment and healing; as well as to invest the time, energy and money that are a tangible demonstration of your commitment to achieving your greatest levels of happiness and fulfillment.

There is much that goes into writing a memoir. It requires courage, strength, commitment and a willingness to share your story so that others may benefit from it in some way. It requires a willingness to reveal the most tender and vulnerable parts of yourself in order to serve others. This is an act of love. Sandra's unique life purpose it to love and be loved. This book is aligned with who she is and why she is here. It is why it had to be written.

The message is this book is relevant for anyone who has ever been in a relationship, who has ever been through major life transitions, who has ever loved and lost and is courageous enough to choose love again.

Sandra's willingness to trust in something greater than herself and to flow with the opportunities that life presents, is a consistent theme throughout this book.

Her ability to honor the challenges and the pain - but not be stopped by them—as well as her willingness to receive help and support from others, are qualities that have served her well. We can all seek to emulate them!

If this book has found its way to you, know that it is not by accident. I believe that the Universe has conspired on your behalf to get it into your hands. Enjoy!

**Helen Macmillan**
Founder & CEO, Helen Macmillan Coaching LLC
www.helenmacmillan.com
April 08, 2018
Maryland

# FOREWORD

M emoirs hold tremendous power to change a reader's life. Even more so when the story is crafted with vulnerability and radical authenticity. Because we are tired of sanitized; we want real, raw, tactile. Spare me from preaching and unsolicited advice, let's have a real conversation. Show me, don't tell me. I want to feel in communion with, held by, gently brought along the path of self-discovery. Let me deduct my own lessons from an analogy, a fable, or a narrative, so that I might embody those nuggets of wisdom and take them as my own.

I met Sandra through a mutual friend and was instantly taken by her fiery soul and her deep heart. Her beauty exudes from the inside out, and anyone who has the chance to be in her presence can feel her resolve. Her gaze on you reminds you that you are worthy of joy, of love, of beauty. She inspires you to love yourself more deeply and to tap into your vast potential.

The way Sandra handles her own trials and tribulations in her memoir encourages the reader to contemplate her own journey. The metaphor of the cuts of a diamond is apt: our experiences shape us, and sometimes experiences that we perceive of as "bad" are ultimately "good." Each bump in the road is the road itself.

Great stories tap into the universal archetypes that have made up all of history and mythology's narratives. Authentic stories gain our trust and invite us to put ourselves in the shoes of a fellow human being. We relate to the essence of their experience, and we transpose their hard-won lessons and wisdom to our own life. As a result, we become closer to one another, closer to the deep humanity that inter-connects us. Sandra's book brings us closer; closer to our own heart, closer to the ones we love, and closer to compassion and forgiveness for the ones who have wronged us.

In her memoir, Sandra embraces all of the facets of life. Her journey of healing and transformation has brought her to a single point focus: uplifting other women on their path to embodied self-worth and real beauty. Although life has led her through painful loss and heartache, she knows how crucially important each experience was for her soul's evolution. Her faith is unshakable, and you will find it empowering to know that she wouldn't change one word of her story, even is she had the chance to make a few rewrites.

The archetype of the "healer" or the "helper" is in all of us. We are all born with a natural desire to connect, to love, to ease pain, and to serve. As we grow up, our experience either brings us closer to this or takes us further from it. Many of us get lost along the way, trying to survive our world, to fit in it, to be seen. But the desire to serve remains within as a primary impulse. Sandra has come out on the other side with this innate impulse still intact. More than that, the spark to support and share has picked up momentum with each heartbreak, and I couldn't be happier that you found yourself somehow in her world. Enjoy the glow.

In Divine Love, always,

**Anne Bérubé PhD**

Author of *Be Feel Think Do: A Memoir*

Hay House

# INTRODUCTION

From a very young age, I was distinctly aware of being different, special—sometimes isolated—but no matter how lonely I felt, there remained this strong connection with God. That feeling of standing out followed me on my travels around the world as a top model, and lingered throughout my marriage to a Jamaican aristocrat, where I sometimes felt like the sacrificial lamb.

I have come to learn what it means to be at peace with myself and feel at home—no matter where my journey takes me. My story from childhood to young adulthood is pretty much the story of the ugly duckling. Ugly was a word I often heard used to describe me as a young girl and so to grow up to become a supermodel was … unexpected to say the least. Sometimes—just plain comical.

I feel very blessed to have lived the life that I lived, and I realize that to anyone looking in from the outside, it might have seemed like a fairytale, but it wasn't. A story without trials or tragedies is incomplete and mine often came in the form of heartbreaks. Something else about myself – I love Love. This made every heartbreak that much more painful, but, instead of becoming disenchanted or giving up on love, I managed to find solace in my broken heart … over and over again, taking each scar as a lesson and following each lesson to spiritual growth and maturity. I guess you can call me a glutton for punishment. With pride I say – better to have loved and lost.

Today I am stronger. Strong enough to share these heartbreaks and show that a woman can be single at 50 without being bitter or hopeless. I still feel chosen to fulfill this purpose —to inspire, and to shine my light where it might be needed—and I still very much love Love, more than ever.

When asked as a child what it was that I wanted to do when I grew up, I gave the same response that I give today. I am writing a book and I will create jewelry—special pieces of jewelry that will mark special occasions and make people smile because of the stories they carry. Today, I share my story to love and honor that little girl that was and is alone with God and the Universe.

> *"When we long for life without difficulties, remind us that oaks grow strong in contrary winds and diamonds are made under pressure."*
>
> Peter Marshall

# CHAPTER ONE
# AGAIN?

**Coming to terms with my new reality—
starting over at almost 50—I finally
listened to the voice inside. Giving him time
to think was the only option left. When I
returned, things hadn't changed.**

---

I never thought I would ever cry like that again. I never dreamed that I would have to suffer such agony a second time. Waves of tears washed my cheeks bare. I found it hard to even stand up straight, as the crippling ache that had taken over my entire body slowly siphoned away my strength. How could I have been so wrong... so blind?

I had just finished unpacking the last of the boxes and the house was finally beginning to feel like home. Construction dust no longer crowded the air and the strong, musty smell had waned somewhat into normalcy. The garden was finally growing out and looked as if it had been kept by some green thumb for quite some time. To think, it had only been five months since we moved in.

Thank goodness for Camilla, my son's girlfriend at the time. She was visiting at the perfect moment – God knows I could not have done it on my own. Camilla coached me through the packing: "Do you want this...?" "Should we pack that...?" but all I could do was nod my head, as it felt like even a single word would drain me completely. Maxine, our housekeeper, tried to console me and begged me to stay calm but even she knew that, for me, it was a hopeless request. Maxine had been there to witness my undying efforts, my sacrifices, and all my trials through the years, all because I had refused to give up on him, on us. Even as she tried to quell my pitiful state, it was apparent from the look in her eyes that she was relieved that I had finally made this decision. She was like a clear thought in the midst of my breakdown, reminding me that this decision was for the best, that I had saved myself from a lifetime of unhappiness and regret. Through Maxine, I could somehow feel the support of everyone who truly cared for me, gathering like strength in my fingers as I packed my life – and what felt like my future—into boxes, like they had no home. I had no home.

The last of my belongings were out the door and on the truck. The only piece left was a painting hanging high above the French doors that lead to the backyard. It was one of my favorites, "Partners in Love." As I made my way down the ladder with the large piece in my hands, I sensed something fall lightly to the floor: the moth. It was dead. I took it as a sign that his work here was done.

It is said that spirits of loved ones sometimes visit in the body of a moth. I had not given much thought to such superstition during my time here in Jamaica, until that day when we received the keys to the new house. I recall walking throughout the empty space, imagining where all our furniture would go, making mental notes of how I was going to decorate our beautiful new home. That day was the first time that the moth made its presence known to me and, every single day since, that moth would be sure to put itself in my view. I knew in my heart that it was my dad. It was as if he was letting me know that I wasn't alone, even though I was so far away from home. He was watching over me. I saw the moth lying lifeless on the floor beneath the ladder and I was certain I was doing the right thing.

It all seems so dramatic when I look back at it and I wouldn't blame you if you thought I was being hysterical but perhaps it would help if you could understand why I was so devastated.

◆

Maybe there is such a thing as being too courageous? It wasn't long after I moved away that I felt strong enough to face again what I had left behind, and we had decided to get back together. Well, I think I had the idea first. I knew I loved Robert and he loved me too, so why let that go to waste? If there was anyone I knew I could count on, it was him. He was smart, kind, funny, affectionate, and clean, all my favorite attributes. When my dad's condition had worsened, he was the first one that I called and he was there for me. You can't just create these experiences with anyone; you can't just form a bond like that with anyone. Robert was there with me through it all. "Have you called hospice?" "Stay strong for your family." "Have you made the funeral preparations?" "Make sure you tell him everything that's in your heart before he passes." Robert guided me every single step of the way.

When the dust had finally settled, I realized that he was too important for me to just let go. "Can you come see me?" I had asked him. I told him that I missed him and that I would like us to talk. He agreed and within a week or so, he had flown up to Miami to be with me. I opened my heart and told him how I felt. He was very clear about the fact that my leaving him left him quite hurt and it would take time for him to fully trust me again. I was willing to do whatever it took to regain his confidence and make us work. We knew that it wasn't going to be easy, but we were both up for the task – or so I thought. We were going to do three simple things: 1) Seek therapy so we could flush out all the old wounds, 2) Discuss the financial expectations, 3) Define our relationship. Where were we headed? Would we eventually get married? When?

I felt like I had another chance at life. What a relief, I wasn't going to be alone! Right then, I set the wheels in motion. That was it, I was moving back and starting a life with this wonderful man. Why? Because he loved *me*. So I began the "returning resident" process. When a Jamaican citizen decides to go back home, they are allowed to take their belongings back duty-free. Still, the process was quite expensive—not to mention tedious—but in no time, I had all the letters, lists, and documents I needed to make it happen. I had seen it in his eyes, felt it in his embrace, and when we were together, nothing and no one else mattered. We would plan our days around music and food. "What are we going to cook today?" was usually our first conversation in the morning. Funny, now that I think about it, that was how it was with my first husband. Wait, my only husband—as you'll see. Anyway, coming from a Cuban family, food was always a deeply meaningful aspect of my experience... the kitchen was where it all happened.

The house was lovely. All my things finally arrived and our new place was perfect! We had a workout room/music room and I even had a space for my office where I could see my clients. We could entertain our friends, Robert's daughter had her own room, and I had a room for my kids, too. Although Adrian and Leah were away at college and most of their belongings were now at their dad's house, I still wanted a space just for them.

I didn't want to bring it up yet. Things were great, why spoil it? So I let some time pass but I was aware that the resentment that he felt towards me for leaving him still lingered. Me leaving was something that he had not yet gotten over. At times, it felt like I was being punished, but because I felt so bad about leaving him and I was desperately afraid of being alone for the rest of my life, I just let it go. Still, my insecurities began to build and before I could see what was happening I was on antidepressants and antianxiety medication, just so I could cope with the loneliness I was feeling.

I uprooted myself; left my family once again all in the name of love and it all blew up in my face. What a surprise. Of course, it was all for the wrong reasons. I convinced myself that things would be perfect. That everything would work out, even though I had no reason to think that it would. Can people change? Not unless they really want to. I was going about it all wrong. The person I needed to love was me. I need to be ok with myself and secure in my own shortcomings but I was depending on him to do it all and when he didn't, when he wasn't willing to take the steps, all I could think was that I wasn't worthy of his love or of any one else's for that matter.

"Mummy, you can't do this anymore. You're so unhappy! I hate to see you like this!"

"I know, my angel girl." That's what I call my precious daughter, Leah. She is my angel, one of my best friends and one of the reasons I do everything in my life. (The other reason is my son, Adrian.)

Leah had that look in her eyes, the one she gets when she feels proud of herself, which is pretty often, as she is a confident young woman.

"I have a great idea! You need a break and some time to think, right?" She knew what was happening. "Since I'm going to Spain for this semester, why don't you go and stay at my apartment in Toronto? It's perfect and love it there."

Of course, it had to be February. When she boarding school, I asked her for one thing and one thing "Please, PLEASE don't make me come see you in Februa It's just way too cold for me, a New Yorker who migrated to the tropics. Still, she was right, it was a great idea.

"You don't even need to pack anything. I have everything you'll ever need," she said.

I waited for the right moment, for us to be on speaking terms. It's no secret that we were both very unhappy.

"I think it is important that you take some time to think. I am going to give you a little space and time to think. When I return you can tell me what it is that you really want." I knew deep inside that it was over. If he let me go, then it was probably a sign that this was something that he didn't want to hold on to.

I was sitting on the plane when I got a message: "Hey, the apartment is available if you want it."

Contrary to what you might be thinking, I didn't reach this stage of my life without learning a thing or two about being prepared for the worst. I had asked some of my close friends in the real estate business to find me a small place. I said it was for an office—Kingston is a very small town and everyone either knows or wants to know your business. Some

here is no doubt about that,

be... curious.

e to Toronto," I replied.

s you can and I'll hold

…ne of my bona fide girlfriends—a former
…o partner—and begged her to send over the money for
me. As usual, she came through without any questions.

I quickly took to cleaning Leah's apartment. She was a student after all, so the place wasn't … let's just say it needed Mama's touch. I rearranged the furniture, cleaned out all the closets and cupboards, and cleaned the kitchen, the bathroom, and everything in-between, all while searching for the chain she lost. It has the letter V for Victoria—my grandmother, and Leah's middle name—and my dad had left it for her when he passed. Ever since I was a kid, I would take to cleaning when I was upset. I also think it was part of my grieving process. There was something cathartic about cleaning.

Sometimes I cried out from sorrow, other times I was just angry, really, really angry. I wasn't about to lose just a partner— I was losing my family, my home, and all the emotion and love I had invested. It felt like my life was falling apart. Everything that I expected to be, all the hopes that I once had, none of it felt valid any longer. I had moved back to Jamaica so that we could move forward together, but now it felt like I had only moved backward and the worst part was, there was nothing I could do about it; I had to just watch it all fall apart and, as shocked as I was that things had turned out the way they did, I knew that I had no choice but to leave it all behind. I felt helpless and hopeless, like I was watching my home burn to the ground.

I had done so much to create that home. When it was time to buy a house, I went looking and found this beautiful home in one of the most sought-after neighborhoods of Uptown Kingston. We took possession of the house in October and wanted to move in by December and I did everything I could to make it possible. We had to move fast, as we didn't want to have to maintain the cost of two homes at once. I was in the middle of rebuilding my jewelry business as I had shut it all down when I left. Rebranded as Sandra Bicknell Personal Jewelry, I launched a website, had a logo designed, and all the advertising material was ready—but I had to put that on hold. I also had a position as Events Coordinator for a media company in Miami that I kept after I moved back to Jamaica. I was able to work remotely but with the time restraints, I could not do it all and our home was the priority. The house needed to be gutted. Although beautiful, it was old and needed remodeling and with my experience in interior design, there was no way we were going to hire someone to do the job. I quickly got a crew of workmen together and the work started. I tore out the kitchen and bathrooms—all the floors and closets, too. I was the interior designer, contractor, and project manager while still playing my role as stepmother and homemaker. I put my all into this relationship and I was steadfast in my focus to make it work. I did my part, I kept my promise, and all I wanted in return was for him to do his part but he refused and the resentment just grew stronger than the love. He had taken away any form of love and affection and basically abandoned me. At that stage, it wasn't just for me. There also was a child in the middle of it as well. His daughter Zoe—whose feelings and wellbeing had to be taken into account—and I had gotten very close. She was just eight years old and I was willing to do anything to avoid hurting her. I reached out to friends and even his family for counseling but no one wanted to get involved. I was desperate, truly desperate, for help but when I found myself alone in the efforts, I was left with no choice but to let it go.

At Leah's home in Toronto, I knew deep in my bones that it was over. For the next three weeks, I came to terms with the fact that I had to leave this relationship. The mere fact that he hadn't as much as called to check on me, much less asked me not to go in the first place, made it very clear that whatever ember had glowed between us had been completely quenched. I spent my days praying, meditating, and exercising. I would go to the spiritual store and stock up on incense, candles, and crystals. I would cry, shower, and cry some more—but not like that time. This time it was just release.

Water is energy and energy is life. You are made up of mainly water; life is created from water and life can be healed from water. Your soul and body crave hydrotherapy as a means of promoting wellness and healing. It's nature's ways of helping you cleanse your mind, body, and soul. By letting tears come to your eyes, whether from laughter or crying, you also let your soul be free and lighter. You release the emotions and let them go through the tears. A shower is like a sacred cleanse for me. I let the water wash away negative thoughts and emotions and send them down the drain.

But the best way to truly console myself was the way I was taught as a child. I must have been two years old when my parents left my sister and me with my uncle to attend to an urgent matter in Mexico. His wife, young and inexperienced, didn't know how to console me, as I cried myself to sleep the first few nights. Out of desperation and pure pity, she thought that teaching me to suck my thumb would bring me a sense of comfort until I was reunited with my parents. Little did she know that I would grow dependent, as it became the way I would console myself throughout my life. Like a companion, my thumb soothes me into a state of meditation by blocking out the pain so I can sort out my thoughts and carve out a plan.

When I got back to Jamaica, there was a tiny sign of change but it just wasn't enough. Like they say, too little too late.

The new apartment was small. I mean really small. I don't recall ever living in such a small space, well, maybe except for that attic apartment in Paris all those years ago. A small apartment might sound like a trifle but when you're nursing heartbreak all the little things seem to accumulate into one sinister villain. Plus it was not where I saw myself at that point in my life. Oh well, it would do. Actually, it was just perfect for just my fluffy little Pomeranian dog, Maxx, and I. The backdoor led from the kitchen to a small patio and a lush little "backyard" where he could run around and do his business without me having to worry about him roaming out of sight. It was safe. I was in the "right" part of town and my landlord, a friend, was just upstairs. My heart was sore and my spirit felt broken, but I was *okay*. I had support, love abundant, and more than anything else, I felt courageous. I made a promise to myself that I would never live another moment unhappy. If it doesn't feel good, if it hurts *at all*, I would get myself out. I admit, it sounded like the makings of a bad habit but it was the truth I was determined to live.

> *"There are some things you can only learn in a storm."*
> JOEL OSTEEN

CHAPTER TWO

# EXPLORING THE LABYRINTH

**Digging deep and doing the work. What am I doing wrong? Why was I making these mistakes and why was I choosing these relationships... or were they choosing me?**

---

O nce you have cried all you can, the only thing left to do is to come to terms with your reality. I had to now face the fact that I was alone, feeling rejected, and facing 50. To top things off, I was living in the basement of a townhouse that was remodeled as a small apartment. To be honest, I thought about it many times in the past: "I hope I don't end up having to live in one of those. What would people think? After all I was Sandra Bicknell." That name probably didn't mean very much since I got divorced but there was a stigma around people's economic standing in that town. I always made sure to maintain a certain standard of living for myself, my children and, admittedly, for all the prying eyes. Yes, I cared about what people thought – but I was starting to see things differently. What mattered most now was the example I set for my children and possibly other women that found themselves in a situation that was far from ideal. So I felt quite proud of myself—I was living in a basement but my life was now on my terms and my terms only

That was when the real work began. I rolled up my sleeves and looked toward a journey of introspection. It was time for some serious self-exploration. I mean, what exactly was going on? I was almost 50 years old and I was still making choices that were not serving me at all... or were they? Not to mention falling for men that were either not available emotionally or just not right for me. I was a riddle I needed to solve.

Where exactly were those wounds? Where did they come from? How were they caused? And the most important question: How was I going to fix it?

Burning incense, praying, and meditating was a good start but I had to go deeper. I often looked to astrology as a way to better understand my personality and why I moved through the world the way I did. I studied my natal chart, had my regular card readings and I also dabbled in systemic constellation—a method of healing the family system. I felt powerfully connected to my spirit guides and, of course, God. I am an Aries and that alone made it all the more difficult. Aries aren't known for their patience but having a Libra rising helped me balance my reactive and impulsive ways.

But astrology was not enough. I had even attended a personal development program, The Landmark Forum, twice and, although some of the techniques they teach are still in my tool kit, I didn't really make the most of it. Fear, as usual, got in the way. I was so afraid of what I would discover. Fear—like they say, ain't nobody got time for that.

I don't remember who suggested it, but Helen's name came up. Of course! Helen knew me so well. She had lived in Jamaica many years before and had been such a source of serenity and healing for me when I was a newlywed. Helen MacMillan was a physical and massage therapist, who became an expert in treating and healing pain. I would see her regularly for my scoliosis, and over time we became kindred spirits. She was also a life coach and so she was the obvious choice to help me. Helen always managed to release some of the sadness I was trying so hard to bury. I trusted her with my life.

I promptly sent her an email and she responded right away. They say that there are no coincidences in life and that has been proven to me time and time again. Helen was going to be in Jamaica right when I felt I needed her. I was going to get to look into her loving eyes and feel her magical embrace, but first I had to figure out how I was going to pay for this.

Oh, I knew I was leaving something out—I also didn't have a job. What's more, I had spent most of my savings on moving back to Jamaica, I was maintaining my apartment in Florida, and I was now paying rent—the icing on my sunken cake. I checked out my bank accounts and I had just enough to cover her fees for the first month. Since she was a friend, she allowed me to pay her month by month. I had already decided that I was doing this no matter what, so I figured I would worry about paying for the rest of the program when the time came.

The journey started and I began to look back at my life in an effort to reveal my deepest self. I found myself facing even more obstacles in the form of memories from my past. However, with Helen's help, I was beginning to see more... to see differently.

Growing up, I was sure that my sister was the family favorite and maybe she was but, as I discovered in one particular session, maybe not to my dad. I recalled a special and tender moment he and I shared that, for many years, had only been a vague and cloudy memory. He lifted me in his strong hands and set me on the mantel in the lobby of our building. I remember feeling terrified. I was certainly not as daring or brave as my sister was. She was fearless. I remember worrying that he was going to leave me there but during that session I recalled the adoring look in his eyes. He looked up at me and he smiled with a gentleness that I rarely saw in my father. He lifted me again, brought me close to him, his grip strong, secure, and gave me a kiss on my cheek. Bit by bit, flashes of memory returned, including one of a ring he wore on his left hand engraved with his name – the one I took the day he passed — that still helps me to reconnect with him when I need him most. With each session, I began to feel lighter and clearer.

As this was unfolding, so was my social life. Little by little, I ventured out of what I called "the dungeon." There weren't many men in Kingston that I felt attracted to. Actually, there were only two—and one had a girlfriend, so realistically, there was only one. It was then that I decided to reach out to "him." Something just came over me, I felt brave and bold. Not really my style but I couldn't help myself or maybe I just didn't want to. I picked up my phone, opened the Facebook app, searched, and found him.

"Hey there!" I wrote. "Was wondering if you wanted to get together, seeing that I'm now single."

I felt my face glow red as a ripe tomato. The chemistry with this guy was always pretty intense. We'd see each other socially but after the cordial greetings, I'd scurry away before anyone would notice that I had the hots for him.

I think it was the very next day that he stopped by for a visit. Just thinking about it now makes me smile a hundred watts. Oh, I liked him so much.

We spent a lovely afternoon together. He was the perfect gentleman. We shared stories about life, likes and dislikes, and of course all the times we saw each other but had to remain calm as I had a boyfriend. Neither of us realized that our feelings were mutually fervent.

Days later, I was offered a position as an interior designer —a career I had a natural aptitude for, as well as some experience—while I was preparing to showcase my jewelry line at

Jamaica's premiere high-end fashion extravaganza; my journey towards self-growth and self-realization had been as revealing as it was fulfilling. I was now looking at life with a new perspective and most importantly my wounded heart was now filled with love and passion again for a man that cherished me. I had moved into my new tiny apartment expecting to have to cope with loneliness and discomfort but—while my views on my living situation had not changed much—I was anything but lonely.

With a new career, new outlook, and a new man, I began to venture more out of "the dungeon" and back out onto Jamaica's social scene. I was sure that this man had come into my life to raise my vibration. He helped me to find a confidence that I hadn't felt in quite some time. I stepped out into the world, a woman revived. I also became a little too busy for my own good. This hit me when Helen cut me loose. The truth is I just couldn't afford it anymore. That's what I told myself anyway. With my journey of self-exploration derailed, my focus shifted from introspective to proactive. I began to delve deeper into the science of astrology to explore whether paying attention to planets and the universe might help me change my reactions, as my road toward unbecoming continued. I wanted to reset and reprogram my thinking and my heart. I began to question everything. Why do we follow all these rules? Who made them up anyway? I knew that all the expectations I had in my past relationships were based on programming and conditioning. Are our emotions real or just a chemical reaction our bodies go through when we find ourselves in a circumstance we believe calls for this response?

It was time to put my philosophy into practice. I pushed myself to love unconditionally and learned to accept my new lover for who he was—a man who had always questioned his own capacity for fidelity. Could I do this? Could I be in a relationship where I would have to turn a blind eye and a blind heart to the reality of his limitations? I had never felt that way about someone before and neither had he. We could not get enough of each other. The spiritual connection was magical, electric, transcendent. One day we were in the car and he reached over to hold my hand. It felt like a lightning bolt shot through my entire body. I was speechless for a moment. It was just delightful. We mirrored each other in a way that was inconceivable. We were convinced that this relationship was meant to be—no matter the obstacle. Infidelity being the one and only potential obstacle, I was sure that we would work... I was sure that I could handle it. I mean, he gave me everything else I ever wanted in a relationship and I mean *everything*. We exchanged ideas, beliefs, religion … we both felt "awakened" because of our love. We felt like home and there was nowhere else we wanted to be. Sometimes it felt so intense that we had to retreat and reassess as we thought it was "too good to be true." I would think about him and he would call. He even had a recurring childhood dream about me. He was sure I was the lady in the shadow with the dark long hair. Yin and Yang was the best way to describe our love; he was the part of me that had been missing all along. Sometimes it even felt irrational but how could it be anything but love when we brought out emotions in each other that felt like they needed to come out in order to heal. As different as we were, we had so many fundamental things in common. This connection was so profound that it could only be destined. We felt like family and that never changed—but his one thing was beginning to stand in the way of us being together. He tried and I don't believe for one minute that it was because of lack of love. At that point, I didn't even care; he was showing me what I most desired.

It was around this time that the novel *The Shack,* by William P. Young, was published. For as long as I could remember, I loved being read to; I guess that's why I love audiobooks. I downloaded *The Shack* and started to listen. The story about God, love, and forgiveness touched me so profoundly that it changed me forever. I was in the kitchen washing the dishes when I got to the chapter where Mack reaches a point of true forgiveness. At that very moment, what felt like a sea of release washed over me. It was as if God himself opened the spout and allowed all the anger and hate I felt to pour out and be washed away with the dishwater. Suddenly all was forgiven. That person, the one that had left me feeling violated as a little girl, the one I hated with all my might, was forgiven. I went through the list of people who had hurt me one way or the other and one by one, I let go of all the ill will that I bore them. I was filled with a love I had never felt before. I can only describe it as jubilation. I sobbed uncontrollably.

Loving him unconditionally is what helped me lose all expectations and that is where the ease came from. But no matter how we both tried, and we did try, I could no longer maintain this secret life. What I didn't tell you is that although we were both two single, consenting adults, we had decided not to share our romance with anyone. We wanted to protect ourselves from any scrutiny, for now anyway. However, I soon learned the hard way that the more some things changed with this one, the more they stayed the same—shocking, right?

Christmas was upon us; a time to be with family and loved ones but not in this case. Just when I thought I'd finally be embraced as someone significant in his life, he was faced with family obligations. Nothing I was unaware of, as we talked about everything. His actions may have been consistent but it sparked a major change in our relationship for me, as I began to question whether or not we would ever be able to have the kind of relationship I wanted. I questioned our commitment and by the time I had gotten to the end of my doubt, I had decided that this relationship was not for me. It was time to let it go, at least the romance anyway—our friendship I will never give up. He came into my life at the most perfect moment. He had scraped me up off the floor of absolute gloom. He encouraged me in all the endeavors I was embarking on and I did the same for him. We loved, respected, and could always count on each other. He was able to read what was on my mind just by the look on my face and I knew when he just needed someone to listen. He calmed me and settled my nerves when

I found myself feeling lost and alone and for that short period, he took the place of my life-long soothing habit. Even though there was that one thing he was not able to give up—I know, I know, you say willing, I say able—he never lied to me and he never promised anything he couldn't deliver. For these things and more, I will be forever grateful. He is one of the most thoughtful, compassionate, and attentive people I know and I will always love him unconditionally, forever connected to him by the delicate Blue Topaz necklace he gave me. A stone of peacefulness, and calming to the emotions, it is ideal for connection with spiritual beings.

I refused to toss this up as just another love affair or dismiss it as another heartbreak. This was different. I did some research, as I love to do, and I found that what felt like a soul mate connection really was more of a twin flame encounter.

The concept of having a "twin flame" originated in Plato's mythic dialogue entitled "The Symposium." In it, he wrote that human beings originally had two faces, four arms, and four legs. Under the threat of being overpowered, the gods split them in half, creating the human as we are today. So it is held that we all have one twin soul out there in the world. Others hypothesize that twin flames are members of our "soul group"—people with whom we resonate with on the deepest level and were predestined to meet—or that twin flames are the embodiment of the other half of a singular soul.

Everything in life is composed of energy at its core, and twin flames are people we resonate with on the deepest spiritual level. Like two tuning forks or gravitational fields, twin flames are magnetically attracted to each other. Twin flames are also our mirrors in that they reflect back to us all of our hidden fears and shadows, but also our true inner beauty and strength. In this way, our twin flames can open the door to tremendous emotional, psychological, and spiritual growth – and so it was with him.

By that time, I had decided that I had had enough of Jamaica. The message from spirit came through the cards and the time was right. The children were now grown—Adrian 23 and Leah 22, still finishing her studies in Toronto.

After 25 years since I first moved there, I felt it was time to make a drastic change. The support was overwhelming. My friends were all rooting for me. Go! This is your time. I went to have my regular chart reading and the planets were aligned.

One night, a group of us decided to go to dinner at the new Japanese place. The conversation was fantastic. We were all talking about all we had been going through and all we had accomplished that day. It was a new moon in Aries and by the end of that night, we all expected to find something special to launch our lives just a little further. When it was my turn, I had nothing to say. I was so upset. "What happened to me?" I asked God as I played with the gold cross on my chain. Nope, nothing had happened that would make any major difference in my life. Not that day anyway.

The waiter approached the table and Kerry said, "Everyone, meet Jordy. He's the one that does all the editing and helps with the content for my social media and media kits for my events."

He said hello and began to update Kerry on all his academic accomplishments.

"So wait, you write too?"

"Yes I do."

What? There it was. My launch. I was going to embark on a new adventure and this time I had decided to share the experience—even the most intimate parts—in my memoir. I was finally going to write a book.

{ *"Your living is determined not so much by what life brings to you as by the attitude you bring to life; not so much by what happens to you as by the way your mind looks at what happens."* }

KAHLIL GIBRAN

# CHAPTER THREE

# I'M NOT A MODEL

**Just coming into my own... my face and spirituality. Realizing that there was a whole world out there that actually thought I was pretty enough to photograph... what a concept. Off to Paris I went.**

---

I was 19 and I still had my braces on. My orthodontist appointments were on the first Wednesday of each month but I hardly ever went. It was my one-day to hang out with my friends after school. My parents were the quintessential Cuban parents, very strict, so we had to be home at 3 p.m. on the dot or my mom would come looking for us. It was NYC after all. Thinking back now, I get it, but back then I thought she was absolutely crazy. I was in my first year of college. I had taken time off but quickly realized that I had to go back to school. I was studying by myself in the study hall when this guy walked in and approached my table. He was really good looking. He had dark olive skin, fine features, and

I remember noticing how manly he was dressed. I remember exactly what he was wearing—a well-pressed dress shirt tucked into a nice pair of slacks with a brown leather belt, loafers, and a dapper Breitling watch. He asked to sit at my table and I gestured with my hand towards the empty chair, already feeling the pull of his charm. We talked about my major and my neighborhood but I realized that throughout our conversation he never stopped touching what I later learned was his brand-new watch. Oh, did he love that watch. For him, it was a symbol of prestige. Day after day, Marc would come sit at my table until he eventually got the courage to ask me out. I, of course, was smitten but oblivious to any deeper attraction on his part. I had braces on, for goodness sake. Plus he was such a man compared to the boys I had dated before. Anyway, Marc and I started dating and a whole new world, a world I had only previously fantasized about, presented itself to my young impressionable mind.

Mark was five years older than I. He introduced me to everyone in the neighborhood. His parents were well-established artists who had been living on Spring Street since before it became a hub for NYC galleries. Marc's was a familiar face everywhere from the grocery below their 6,000 sq. ft. loft, to all the bars and restaurants in his neighborhood, and he was loved by all; he was the Johnson's son, after all. Marc exposed me to a whole new world that I had only glimpsed on TV, a world where Andy Warhol, Keith Haring, and the Beastie Boys were friendly with the guy I was dating. I felt something like his Breitling watch, a prized possession he would showcase on his arm. "Hi, yes, this is my girlfriend Sandra." It was kind of funny. I had never received that kind of attention before. I finally took off the braces because I didn't want to look like "the little girl on Marc's arm". Marc's world definitely wasn't the braces scene, much less suited for a thumb-sucker. I had to get rid of that habit. The truth is, I didn't need it, not then anyhow. We went to glitzy parties and dinners at high-end restaurants. Occasionally we would even travel to the family home in St. Lucia where Mr. Johnson spent half the year because he was so over the NYC art scene.

When I mentioned I was looking for a job, Marc suggested I apply at Detour, a men's boutique on West Broadway in Soho. It was right around the corner from where he lived so it was perfect, even though it was practically the last stop on the E Train, exactly one hour away from my station. I remember thinking how different the Spring St. Station was from Elmhurst Ave., my station all the way in Queens. It was like I entered the train at a middle-class suburbia and got off in the upper echelons of a modern metropolis.

I would go to school all week, NY Tech in Columbus Circle, then work in Soho on Wednesdays and weekends. I'd usually stop at the phone booth just at the top of the station right before I started work. One day I made my usual call to Marc but he sounded different and I could tell something was wrong. He could barely form the words to tell me the news. He was leaving New York. His grades were way below his parents' expectations. This wasn't the first warning but it was the last. In fact, it wasn't a warning at all; they were not joking around, his bags were packed, and he was set to leave in a few days. I was devastated to say the least. We had been together for two years and had become inseparable. My routine was school, work, and home, and Marc occupied all the free time I had in between. I didn't have many friends because I spent morning, noon, and night submerged in Marc's life.

"Second floor, please."

I was getting into the elevator on my way to typing class, when my classmate, Ryan, barreled through the closing doors.

"Sandra, I need you to do me a huge favor," he bargained. "I have a photography presentation due next week and I need you to model for me."

"No way! I am not a model. I wouldn't even know what to do. I'm sorry but I can't." Was this guy kidding me?

"I have no one else. It's for school. Pleeeeease." Ryan wouldn't take no for an answer, until finally I agreed to help him.

I borrowed clothes from Detour's sister store and went over to Ryan's house one Saturday afternoon. He had set up a background—a grey cloth on the back wall of his living room. I put on the first outfit and sat on the floor where he had drawn a big "X". I posed, recalling how my dad would position my sister and I for photos when we were kids. Whenever my mom dressed my sister and I in our pretty dresses, my dad would sit us down on the sofa, or in the lobby, and take pictures of us. He would adjust our clothes, fix our hair and straighten our heads until we looked just perfect. I think we got about five or six shots before Ryan exclaimed, "It's a wrap!" He was truly grateful and I was truly happy to help.

A few weeks later, I bumped into Ryan and his friend Chris in the vestibule of our school building.

"Can you meet me in the Library at 3? I have something I need to show you."

"Sure, I'll see you then."

"What's your problem, Chris?" He was making this funny face that I couldn't quite decipher.

"Nothing," he said and off they went.

I walked into the library and Ryan was sitting at a table by himself. I walked over and sat right across from him.

"What's up?"

He pushed a black report folder across the table towards me.

"I made this for you," he said.

I flipped to the first page, then the next and the next. It was all me, page after page. Ryan had created a portfolio of me.

"Sandra, you have to become a model."

I was still looking at the photos. I could not believe my eyes, much less my ears. Sure, they were some nice pictures but...

"Absolutely NOT! Are you kidding me?"

"Please, please, Sandra. You can do it. You are beautiful!" he said.

"Get out of here. I am not a model!!!!" I repeated. "Come on let's go, I have to go home."

We left the library and when we got to the lobby, there was Chris with that same expression. This time I understood why he was looking at me like that.

"No!" I said, before he opened his mouth.

"Sandra, come on. At least give it a try."

It went on like this for days until finally I caved.

"Fine! Find the closest agency to school. I'll go to that one and if they say no, we drop this silly idea. OK????"

They both nodded and high-fived, at which I rolled my eyes. Aside from the fact that I did not think I was model material, I really didn't feel like facing rejection either. I was still heartbroken about Marc's departure, so my spirits were low enough already. The closest agency happened to be Click Agency on 5th Ave., just a few blocks away from school. I walked into the busy office, which had one big, round table set in the middle of the room with about eight people sitting around it and they all seemed to speak a different language. The environment was lively, phones were ringing constantly, it seemed like big deals were being made.

"Hi, I'm Sandra. I have an appointment?" I felt so out of place.

"You have a book?" The receptionist asked and I handed her my report folder of pictures.

"How tall are you?"

"5' 7"," I replied.

"Ok, you can come back in an hour."

Ryan, Chris, and I went to the coffee shop downstairs and waited for what felt like an eternity before we went back up, me with an awful feeling in the pit of my stomach. I already knew what they were going to say and although I was quite happy not to become a model, a tiny, little, itsy part of me was hoping she would say, "Yes, sign on the dotted line."

"I'm sorry but we're not interested in your look at the moment," she said, just as expected, as she handed back my "book."

It wasn't even about my height. It was my look they weren't interested in and who could blame them. I had short dark hair with androgynous features and although I was slender, I was just not model material.

"Satisfied?" I faced Ryan and Chris.

"Ah, they don't know what they are talking about," Ryan spoke but Chris kept quiet.

It turned out that Click was one of the top agencies in the city with several top models on their roster.

It was Wednesday so I had to go to work. That train ride was never the same after Marc left. I had become a completely different person when I was with him. He brought out in me a confidence I never even knew I had.

I was putting my things away in the employee closet when Elsa arrived.

"Look," I said, "I brought the pictures." I had told her all about Ryan and Chris's plan.

"Oooo, let me see."

I left her with the pictures and started my shift. About halfway through the day, she confronted me.

"Sandra, I want you to meet David and Linda. They run Boy Girl Models. They'd like to meet you."

"Why would they want to meet me?"

But Elsa didn't have time for my clueless questions. She pulled me by the hand over to where a strikingly debonair man and an attractive woman were standing and made the introduction.

"This is Sandra."

"Hi Sandra, we'd like you to come to the office tomorrow so we can set up a test shoot."

"Sure," I smiled.

"What in the world is a test shoot?" I asked Elsa after they left.

"They want you to do a shoot with the photographer so you can build your portfolio. They want to sign you, Sandra."

The test went well. I must have gotten some really nice pictures because, before I knew it, I was confirmed on a direct booking to Paris. Yup, just like that I had to wrap my head around the fact that I was heading to Paris to model. Me. Model! In Paris!

I had to sit my parents down and explain it all. It all happened so fast that I can barely remember the details but what I do remember is what my dad said to me: "You go, Sandra. This kind of opportunity comes once-in-a-lifetime and I sure can't afford to send you to Paris, so go."

Ryan and Chris weren't the least bit surprised when I broke the news to them. If Ryan had not asked me for that favor, if he hadn't printed those pictures for me and encouraged me, my story would've turned out quite differently. So thank you Ryan and Chris—I will be eternally grateful.

"Now, I have to go shopping!" I thought.

I was going to Paris, after all. I did some research, observed the models and how they were dressed when they went into the agency, and with the help of Elsa, I put a wardrobe together. I was on the hunt for a special pair of cowboy boots when I noticed a sign advertising psychic readings. I made an appointment and went to glean my fate. The psychic told me that I was going to have a fruitful career. Exactly what I needed to hear! She went on to add that I was going to marry and have two children, a boy and a girl. She also said, "Keep wearing that brooch. It will bring you luck," and that it did. It belonged to my mother but I wore it all the time. The most interesting information she gave me was that I would be most successful when I was 53 years old. I was happy about everything she had to say, but I had to wait till I was 53 for my success? She spoke with such conviction as if she had known me my whole life. She said many things but that one thing stuck in my head all these years.

All the arrangements were made and I was off to Paris. The taxi left me in front of these big old doors. I walked up two flights of stairs, went through another set of tall doors and there it was again, a big round table with people sitting around it, speaking all different languages, making deals. And that's when it hit me: I am a model. I was a "City" model, the top women's agency in all of Paris, back in the day when models were celebrities, not the other way around. Marc and I stayed in touch as much as we could but after some time, it became more and more difficult to maintain this long-distance relationship. I was so busy it was impossible for me to go see him and he was definitely not able to come to Paris to see me. His parents were not having it.

I was working all the time. After a few weeks in Paris, I was booked to shoot a catalog in Guadeloupe. That's where I met Angie. We were sharing a room and became instant friends. She was so beautiful and smart but what intrigued me the most about Angie was that she was very spiritual. She asked me my sign and it turned out she was an Aries too.

Not only was she spiritual, she was also an empath: a highly sensitive soul.

"You are going to do so well, Sandra. I can see it; you're going to do all the covers."

Although I was a model, I still didn't understand what people were talking about. Anyway, I was happy to meet Angie; she was fun. We flew back to Paris and I was booked to work every day. The editor of Elle magazine in particular really liked me. That's where I got the nickname "La Petite."

I hadn't been feeling well since I got back from Guadeloupe. My head was hurting, my body was aching but I had to keep going. I couldn't turn down these jobs. I went to the studio for a job with Tyen, who regularly shot for Dior and Vogue. Most models would've killed for that job and I thought I was going to die on that job. Every time the flash went off it felt like an explosion went off in my head. I asked to go home early that day which is unusual for me. I actually believed that one of the reasons I was worked so much was because I was so easy to work with. I never went on with any antics as many of the other models did. I arrived on time and did as I was told.

The next day I was set to shoot a spread for Elle magazine. The alarm went off but I could not get up. I could not move my arms nor my head and I could barely open my eyes. The light was way too bright. When I didn't show up, the agency called to ask what was wrong. When they heard the symptoms they rushed over with an ambulance and rushed me to the hospital.

I had been in Paris for just a few months but I understood everything the doctors were saying. I had meningitis. It seems I had picked it up while in Guadeloupe. I had two spinal taps and spent a couple of weeks in the hospital. The girl I shared the hospital room with was flown in from Guadeloupe as well. Unfortunately, she didn't make it. One morning I woke up and her bed was empty. Was I going to die, too? Was I going to die all alone in a hospital bed in Paris, so far away from home?

These were the questions that consumed my waking moments. I always had a close relationship with God though, so, strangely enough, I felt at peace. I just knew that He would take care of me—I knew that his will would be done – and I also had tremendous faith that I was going to be okay. In time, I recuperated and after a couple of weeks I was released from the hospital. It was two more weeks until I regained my strength and to my surprise, after that grueling month, Elle magazine had waited for me to shoot. After that, I worked with all the top photographers, did all the top campaigns. Oliviero Toscani for Benetton, Robert Erdman for Equipment, and Elle Magazine with Walter Chin, Pamela Hanson, Ellen Von Unwerth—I even shared the cover of Vogue, shot by Albert Watson. Oh yes... and the International Gap campaign. That one was even cooler because my sister was the manager at a Gap store when the campaign was released. My mom and sister had these massive posters saved for me. I actually had them until just three years ago. The ugly duckling was on the cover of Cosmopolitan UK twice and Marie Claire, Spain. Those were a few of the jobs I landed during my career. I think everyone was a bit surprised at my success, especially me.

Angie and I remained friends. She taught me all about astrology, crystals, fairies, and meditation. Angie called herself a witch and I believed her. Sometimes I would go visit her and the door would be open. "I knew you were coming. Do you want some tea?" That's where my interest in the spiritual blossomed—yet another tool that has helped me cope and find comfort through the ebb and flow of my life.

> *"And then Magic said, I will place in your path guides to help you remember love when all seems lost. These guides will love and protect you, and they will teach you to fly."*
>
> NAUSICAA TWILA

CHAPTER FOUR
# WHEN AGAIN?

**Swept off my feet like a princess? Set up
by mutual friends, we fell in love.
My hero had arrived, or was I his?**

---

I n the 1990s, Miami was synonymous with high fashion
and the expanding modeling industry. Ocean Drive's
Art Deco buildings were a regular backdrop for glossy
magazines and European catalogues. By day, photo shoots
blocked the streets of Ocean Drive; by night, the Miami
club scene was introducing the "House Music" movement.
After my three-year stint between Paris, New York, London,
and Tokyo, I decided to give Miami a go. It was the natural
progression for most models and modeling agencies from
every corner of the industry. Although I was now part of the
"top model" pack, I didn't live like the typical models did. I
managed to stay grounded as best I could. Drugs and partying
were just not part of my lifestyle.

One coincidence after the other seemed to keep me within a wholesome environment. Of course, I don't really believe in coincidences. My journey was paved, as it is for all of us, since the day I was born. I believe that we are presented with situations, opportunities, and circumstances throughout our entire lives and what we choose to do with them is up to us. The choices we make determine our accomplishments here in this life. I say accomplishments because I believe our purpose in life is to serve.

"I have the perfect guy for you," said my friend Nicholas as we walked towards the beach. Blaise, Mo, and Neil followed behind.

Nicolas was from Jamaica and so were the others. The ones who can afford it send their children to study abroad and, because of its proximity to the island, Miami was perfect. I had visited "the rock," as natives like to call it, a few months before with Blaise. I was a guest at his family home in Montego Bay the previous summer. Blaise had created an adventure tour around the island and wanted to show me as much of its beauty as possible. From Montego Bay, we made our way through the South Coast, making a quick stop at his Mimi's house; what a house that was. It sat on three acres of the most enchanting grounds with what seemed like every type of flower and fruit tree imaginable. Mrs. Desnoes – Blaise's grandmother, and the widow of Mr. Desnoes of Desnoes and Geddes (the brewers of Jamaica's world famous Red Stripe Beer) – was an elegant, stately woman with a strong British-Jamaican accent. She was also one stern lady. From there, we headed up to their cottage in Blue Mountain. It was one spectacular view after the other, as we drove up the mountain. Flying past the steep cliffs as we skirted the road's edge, Blaise pointed out the marvel that is Jamaica. Day after day, we visited the most scenic and magical corners of the island. Port Antonio, Ocho Rios, Negril then back to Tryall near Montego Bay where our tour concluded, and another adventure began in the form of a four-day music festival called Reggae Sunsplash. The villa where we stayed was filled with some of Blaise's closest friends and family, including boxer Lennox Lewis when his career was just about to soar. Twenty-five years later, most of the people there have remained intimate friends and practically family to me.

"You guys would really hit it off. David Bicknell. Don't you know him?" Nicholas went on.

Although an unusual name, it did sound familiar. It took some time before I could recall that I had been introduced to a David Bicknell on my visits to Jamaica. It was a fleeting moment, too brief to measure first impressions.

Days later, I got a call early one morning, "Sandra, you must come over for Sunday lunch."

It was Nicholas' sister.

"Susie, you know I don't drive. How am I going to get there and, an even better question, how am I going to get home?" I had so many doubts.

"Just get here and we'll figure out the rest."

"Ok, I'll make my way," I replied.

Pinecrest was pretty far from South Beach where I lived. A friend happened to be going to that side of town, so I caught a ride with her. I had no idea that this was a set-up – a blind date. David was there! He was visiting for the weekend. We all sat down for lunch and suddenly we found ourselves alone. He was packing to head back to Jamaica that night. I had to stop myself from staring into his mesmerizing, hazel-green eyes. I had never seen a man with lashes as long as his. All my days in the modeling industry, I had never laid eyes on such a handsome man. He resembled MacGyver from the TV series but sorry, David left him in the dust when it came to looks *and* charm. Turns out, he was my ride back to South Beach on his way to the airport. We sat close to each other in the back seat of the car. The energy! The chemistry! It was palpable.

"When again?" he whispered as we arrived on my street.

I had no idea. I couldn't think past that very moment. The romance ensued quickly and feverishly. We were in love. He visited me in Miami and I him, every chance I had.

His dad joked, "You'd think David had shares in Cable and Wireless and Air Jamaica," because of how often we spoke over the phone and the frequent trips we took to see each other. I was introduced to his family and friends right away. Most were incredibly warm and welcoming, but others were suspicious of my motives. Yes, they had a lovely home and a gorgeous beachfront villa on the north coast of the island but

I didn't really understand the extent of their wealth at that time. Modest and understated with strong family values, the Bicknells never exhibited their affluence. I suppose I don't blame those who questioned my interest in him since he was the youngest of three and with his mom ailing, some thought he was at his most vulnerable, and he was. I too wanted to love and protect him so at that time it was hurtful that they thought that way, as we were genuinely head over heels in love with each other.

David's buddy once walked over to me and asked, "Can I speak with you a moment?"

Sure, I didn't think much of it and went for a drive with him.

"What are your intentions? Do you realize that if you ever marry him you'd have to become a Jamaican? Your life would be here, forever. Are you prepared for that type of commitment?"

We had been together just three months and although we had spoken about marriage, all we thought about was spending every waking moment together. As I tell the story now, having a 23-year-old son of my own, I can honestly say that I understand why they would have such concerns, but then, I was horrified and humiliated. It was his family however, that quickly came to my defense and the support was overwhelming.

My career had reached a plateau and it was time to recharge and redirect. At that point in my career, I was faced with a choice: I would either head back to Paris or forge a career in acting and head to Los Angeles where I had an agency waiting to represent me. I had no desire to do either. All I wanted was to be with the man that I called "my hero." He had swept me off my feet like Cinderella. I made a commitment and was due to go back to Tokyo. I was offered a contract that I had to honor and I also needed the money. The idea of us being apart for a month was devastating to say the least, but I had to go.

Every day after each shoot I would rush to the agency before they closed, and every day there was a fax, more like a love letter, from David. I still have every single one of them. I was on the other side of the planet but that didn't stop our unmitigated romance. He would fax me, I would fax back, and the romance continued to blossom. Absence made my heart grow fonder. The month could not move fast enough. I loved Tokyo—one of my favorite cities in the world. I have been to many but Tokyo still holds a special place in my heart. A city that's equal parts perplexing and alluring, Tokyo thrills most visitors. I could actually go on a tangent about this magical place but there is so much left to this story, I must stay on track.

The four weeks were finally over and I was back in my hero's arms. After I landed, we headed directly to the villa to join the family. I was so happy to see him, I could not keep my hands off him, it just felt so great to have him right there with me, in the flesh. I held his hand, rubbed his shoulder then his chest, but he shrugged my hand off. I found that odd but didn't make much of it.

"I've been thinking," he said, "maybe you should consider moving to Jamaica so we can see how it goes. We can live together for a while and go from there."

First of all, my family would not approve. Although I had been basically on my own for the past four years, I was very close to my family and had the utmost respect for my parents. For a conservative, catholic, old-fashioned Cuban family with traditional values, living together before marriage was not an option. I could not believe my ears. I immediately went into a temper.

"What are you talking about?"

I was not expecting this cool and casual reception. Something was terribly wrong. They got to him, I thought. While I was away, someone got to him and made him reassess our future plans.

"You know what? If this is what you're really thinking maybe I should just go right back to the airport."

I was not having it. As I turned to him to continue my rant, I noticed something shiny in his hand. It was a beautiful diamond set in yellow gold, an engagement ring. He had it in his front pocket, hence the shrug. I could not believe my eyes. He was proposing right then and there, in the car. I was so upset by the way he was speaking, his cold response, so to ease my distress he was left with no choice but to propose in the car while driving. One of the happiest moments of my life. Unbeknownst to me, he had asked my dad for my hand in marriage some time before my arrival.

Mrs. Bicknell's health continued to deteriorate so the wedding plans went on full speed ahead. There was no time to waste. She wanted to be sure her baby was happy and settled before the inevitable occurred. Invitations, caterers, wedding planner, all ready to go. All decided before I could blink an eye, the wedding was scheduled and basically on autopilot.

"You'll be married on June 20th."

My wedding was three months away. They had the wherewithal to make things happen with a snap of the fingers. It was a very difficult time for the family. Mrs. Bicknell, a charitable and adored member of society, was also a highly influential person. David and I were overwhelmed. Yes, we so desired to be married but this was happening way too fast and we hardly had any control. The invitation list carried 600 names. No, that was not a typo. Six hundred invited guests of which I knew possibly 50 at the time. With David's Jewish mother and Anglican father, neither practicing, I wouldn't have the Catholic wedding I always assumed I'd have, and with the situation, the wedding would have to be in Jamaica. I loved him so much that I was willing to go with whatever was presented and to be quite honest, we didn't have a moment to even think about it.

The house was buzzing with excitement, with an undertone of sadness all at once. Mrs. Homi, a family friend, and her daughter Lisa came to pay Mrs. Bicknell a visit and I was called to meet them as they sat around her bed reminiscing on old times as well as, of course, the upcoming festivities. We bonded quickly.

"We'd like to take you to lunch one of these days, perhaps assist with your bridal registry?" they asked.

I don't think I even knew what that meant. My parents being Cuban immigrants of simple means, I was quite sheltered, so these conversations were not exactly common in our household. When I said "Cinderella," I meant it.

A few days later, Mrs. Homi, Lisa, and I made our way through every home accessories and bridal store in Kingston, all four of them. In those days, Jamaica was limited when it came to retail shopping.

"Choose, Sandra, what do you like?"

The prices were not an issue, what was important was that I selected enough. With the ladies guiding me as to what I *must* have in my new home, I pretty much had every type of glass, platter, serving cutlery, and linen imaginable. Paintings, mirrors, even furniture. Before we knew it, the house was filled with gifts. Every table, room, and corner had gifts piled up. A sight to see. Each gift was wrapped more beautifully than the other. I could not believe my eyes.

"These are all for us?" I questioned with excitement.

"Yes, they are. All of them," said David.

The wedding day was fast approaching and with Mrs. Bicknell's condition deteriorating, as you can imagine, the tensions were high. Friends and family began to arrive from all corners of the world to witness this occasion, but also to bid farewell to the beloved matriarch that was Mrs. Bicknell, the epitome of Jamaican Royalty. The day that was meant to be the happiest day of my life became a form of comfort and distraction from the elephant in the room – the fast approach of the loss of my hero's mother, his heroine. David would not make any decision without consulting his mother. Her eyes would light up when he walked into the room and he melted when in her presence. Always a tender exchange between the two and a bond every mother and son could only hope for. For Mr. Bicknell, steadfast in his garden walks, methodical and meditative in his tool room, his children were his universe, an orderly one. His energy was so powerful, you had to be clear with your words and actions, lest you get a bark which could feel like a bite and on those particular days leading up to the wedding, he was a man filled with purpose—but you could see the sorrow in his eyes and even in his actions, which sometimes came across as irrational.

As I tell this part of my story, I pause to take a breath and shed some tears, as I remember that young, naive, genuinely good girl. I am filled with love and compassion for her. I hold her in my memories and send her a hug.

The stress finally took its toll. My back went into spasm and I was unable to move a muscle without excruciating pain.

The doctor came to examine me with his physician's bag, just like in the olden times.

He stated, "This woman is under severe stress and must rest."

I had suffered the same issue while trekking through Thailand just a year before, but this time was different. It wasn't caused by a heavy backpack and walking miles through the gorgeous jungles of Chiang Mai. This was caused by the express train to maturity I had boarded. You see, this chapter in my life was the most difficult. You know what they say about hindsight, and although I've thought about it time and time again, there is something quite different when it comes to writing about it. It was supposed be the happiest time of my life, of our lives, but the fact remained, it was the saddest time for the Bicknell family. It was a clear example of my time to serve. This situation chose me and I chose it. I clearly had a lot to learn, as I discovered through the years that followed, but at that moment, it was a time to hold the space for some who desperately needed joy.

The wedding was spectacular to say the least. The flowers, the food, and all the guests that came from far and wide made what was otherwise a somber time, a celebration of life. With the blessings from God above, the torrential rain was also what made it even more special. My family, just the handful that were able to attend, also had the time of their lives. Not my mother, she saw it all crystal clear. She adored David and his family, but she knew that her little girl was in for a rude awakening. Even though she was never one to intrude and was always supportive, my mom spoke her mind then allowed us to make our own decisions. She herself was 25 years old when she left Cuba to join my father in New York City. Ironically enough, Jamaica was where she stayed before making her way to her husband in America. During the reception, my mom approached two of Mrs. Bicknell's best friends, Beverly Rousseau and Mrs. Kelly. With her New York-influenced yet thick Spanish accent she begged each of them to keep an eye on me. She took my hand and placed it in theirs and said, "Please care for her and consider her your daughter in my absence."

People began to leave. It was still relatively early when I realized they had just gone home to change into something comfortable, only to return to what became a full-fledged party. To this day, 25 years later, people still remember that special day. They either say, "Hi, we met at your wedding," or "Your wedding was the best I'd ever been to."

Halfway into our honeymoon, we were called back into Kingston. We saw that Mrs. Bicknell's health had taken a turn for the worst as she had fallen into a coma. We hadn't gone far, as this was expected. The winding road leading back to Kingston felt like an eternity, even though David was driving at top speed. I could feel the heaviness of his sorrow. He knew the end was near. We had only known each other just eight short months that felt like a lifetime and most of that time was spent planning a wedding, our wedding, around the little time Mrs. Bicknell had left. Any complaint, desire, or questioning on my part was dismissed as insignificant, as the looming loss of a loved one trumped all. I spent those months walking a tightrope most of the time. Ironically enough, I felt like an intruder during such an intimate and personal time in these people's lives, people I hardly knew, who barely knew me. Mrs. Bicknell died 10 days later.

It was just the two of us in this big townhouse filled with family antiques and boxes upon boxes of gifts waiting to be stored away. I sat for days writing hundreds of thank you cards to people. I couldn't put a face to a name. "Dear Mr. and Mrs. Stranger, thank you very much for the lovely Wedgewood vase. It will match perfectly in our living room. Our best, David and Sandra."

Each day, I learned another formality that was quite foreign to me. As foreign as Ackee and Saltfish, the Jamaican national dish, and their native tongue, Patois – I was so lost and so very lonely. David tried so hard to make things easy for me. But how could he? He himself didn't know much about being a newlywed either. The strain on our marriage pretty much began right away. David was just 27 years old and he no longer had his doting mother to coddle him. Family members would come to visit, check on us, and occasionally take me out so I could learn the city, but we were just two big kids playing house. Would we have gotten married so soon after meeting if the circumstances were different? Would we have even stayed together? We never even had a chance to find that out.

But here we were. I had to become Mrs. Bicknell, run a home, lead the staff, and entertain dutifully. What in the world did I know about all that? Not one thing. I didn't even know how to drive. Each day after David would go off to work, I would take the car down the road, a little further each day until I taught myself how to get around Kingston. Anita, my sister in law (well, actually she was David's sister in law, she was married to David's brother Chris), would draw me maps, including pictures of landmarks, so I would learn my way around town without getting lost. The two of us, slim with dark, short hair, became thick as thieves. There was nothing we wouldn't do together, but not even that would help alleviate the pressure David and I both felt. What a predicament we were in.

A year later, in fact on our one-year wedding anniversary, I discovered I was pregnant with Adrian. We were overjoyed, as we had suffered a miscarriage a few months earlier when I was about 10 weeks pregnant. I had been spotting for a few days and the doctor suspected I had an ectopic pregnancy so I was rushed to the hospital for surgery. It turned out I was misdiagnosed and the aggressive surgery was too much for the little fetus. It was the third world after all and the technology was a little behind, to put it gently.

Adrian was born 7 weeks early weighing 7 lbs. 9ozs. Our bundle of joy had blond hair and chubby little cheeks. He was precious and just like that, "Super Dad" was unleashed. Changing diapers and rocking him back to sleep, David was enchanted with his son and first born. Seventeen months later, Leah joined us. She had strawberry blonde hair and tiny little lips. Chris's nickname for her was "Tweedy Bird." I had two, under two. Susie, my sister, and I are 14 months apart, and I wanted my children to be close in age as well.

Leah suffered with terrible colic and with Adrian being just 17 months old and me with a severe case of postpartum depression, it was decided that I would spend some time at the country home where I would benefit from extra support. Joanne, David's sister, was visiting from Florida and helped me as much as she could; after all, she was already a pro with three kids of her own—a set of twins and a young boy. Joanne, eight years David's senior, was the epitome of the perfect mother. Grateful and intimidated at the same time, I had tremendous respect for the new matriarch of the family but sometimes it proved to be too much, as again I found myself always falling short. At least that's how I felt.

David tried all he could to make the marriage work but with his shortcomings and my insecurities, it was a recipe for disaster.

I was brushing my teeth one night and my little angel girl walked into the bathroom; she was just two and a half at the time. She put one hand on the vanity counter, crossed her little leg and put her other hand on her hip.

"What you doing, mummy?"

I remember this as clear as day. Right there in that very moment I looked in the mirror and, to my dismay, I noticed I resembled my mother more than ever: the sadness in her eyes, the way her eyelids drooped. I looked back at Leah and instantly I knew that I could not, would not let the cycle of sadness continue. I was not passing this down to my daughter. Shortly after that, David and I separated.

Mr. Bicknell, also cursed by cancer, passed shortly after that. To bear the things he bore with as much grace as he did, always coming out stronger, undefeated, was a mark of David's strength. That was the David I married and I know that he is the same David now. No matter his limitations and my deficiencies, the circumstances proved to win over love. We did our very best—I say that with all the compassion in the world for those two young people who only wanted to share a life together. Alone and at opposite sides of the ring, we picked our divorce attorneys. Friends and family each picked a side and that is when things began to get ugly. Even though it started as a peaceful decision, ego, fear, anger, and resentment—all the same unconscious devil, all based on conditioning and programming—began to creep in. Although the intentions were pure and for our best interest, the whispers, egging on and advice coming from all directions really got the volcano rumbling. It was the talk of the town as most people were shocked at the news. The fairytale marriage came crumbling down and when it did, it was a free-for-all. Divorcing from such a powerful family proved to be the most frightening time of my life. Just weeks after he moved out, my citizenship papers arrived, sending a clear message, "You will *not* leave Jamaica with my children." That was exactly what the family feared pre-nuptials, and it was clear that it was going to get even uglier. I struggled with a host of emotions: fear, sadness, and utter failure. I again found myself curled up with my thumb, day after day after day, as I fought off overwhelming depression. I thought about it for an instant but quickly decided that there was no way that I would leave Jamaica with the children. What right did I have to take someone's children away? What right did I have to separate these children from their father? None. I was an adult, I made the decision, and it was no fault of theirs that it didn't work out. The two of us were represented by the mightiest divorce lawyers on the Island; the meetings became quite combative, to say the least. David wanted to be fair, there was no doubt about that, but the powers that be had different intentions. Fair is objective, isn't it? We finally settled out of court and David made sure the kids had everything they needed.

The children, Adrian four and Leah three, didn't understand much of what was going on. To some degree, that was the reason we decided to part ways at that stage. It would be easier on them. That's what we thought anyway. As I sit here on the plane heading to Florida for Christmas with my family, writing this very book, I can recall each occasion where that was not the fact. It was far from easy for them. They became tired of the back and forth from Mummy and Daddy's house. Where was home? The days when they'd fall sick and wanted both of us close; vacations with Dad and homework with Mom; their lives became a split screen.

We did not want our children to grow up in a volatile and loveless environment. One thing I believe to be as certain as my name is Sandra—God gives us the lessons we need at the time we need them in order to best serve others, when appointed. There is no escaping karma and the molding of each one of us and our life's purpose.

{ *"Let go or be dragged."*
ZEN PROVERB }

# CHAPTER FIVE

# THE LITTLE VOICE INSIDE

**When the perfect life fell apart... the time had come for me to go, too. A divorce and a 10-year relationship later, I had to start all over again. But first, I had to get my ego in check, scrape myself off the floor, brush myself off, and gracefully rise again.**

---

**N**egril, home of the famous Seven Mile Beach— miles of white sand and turquoise waters—is an intoxicating spot. This little piece of heaven is meant for relaxing, partying, and taking in good vibes. Maria and I had driven down for the weekend and decided to make Margaritaville our last stop before heading back to town. As we made our way to the parking lot, I noticed her waving to the brown-skinned, bald-headed guy that rode in on a motorbike as we loaded up the car.

"That's my cousin," she said as she pointed him out.

There was something so incredibly familiar about him. I was instantly drawn to him but I didn't think he noticed me that day. Immediately after we got in the car I began to question Maria about her charming cousin.

"Come on, give me the rundown. What's his name?"

"Sandra, you have to trust me. Jeremy is not for you," she said with a knowing smile, her light brown curly locks and beautiful freckled face making her seem that much more radiant.

Despite Maria's free-spirited ways, one of her many endearing qualities, she was adamant that Jeremy and I were totally incompatible. Maria and I had been friends since I moved to Jamaica. It had been six years at that point, and so I trusted her judgment even though I remained curious.

It turned out that Jeremy had noticed me after all and had asked Maria for my number. When he called, I cringed. I did not want to speak on the phone with him before I met him formally in person. You see, I had a thick New York accent with a certain nasal quality, which made the comparison to Fran Drescher's character in *The Nanny* irresistible to many Jamaicans. I answered the call and made it as quick as possible.

"Sure, tomorrow? I'd love to go for a drink. Ok, bye," the conversation was over before I could feel even more self-conscious. Shortly thereafter, Jeremy and I began dating. It was a little tricky at first; I did have two small children. Jeremy was just 23 and I was 30. I know, talk about cringe-worthy, but there was something different about him. He seemed quite mature for his age and I have always appeared and come across as a lot younger. Even as a model, although I was 21, the agencies always told me to say I was 18. I guess that was why I was able to keep my wits about me, seeing that I was a bit older than my peers. Jeremy would often visit on weekends and the children began to grow attached to him.

"Stay! Stay!" they asked him one evening.

He hadn't spent the night yet as I wanted to be sure they were comfortable before I allowed him to stay over. After some time, Jeremy and I became more and more serious and over time, we became like a family. We had an amazing relationship, two peas in a pod. A team.

Jeremy and I would travel often and entertain a lot and David was more than happy to take the kids when we did. David worshipped them, so the more time he had with them, the better. We had joint custody but Adrian and Leah lived with me. They would go to their dad's every other weekend and every Wednesday but because of the close proximity, we basically shared custody. David quickly remarried and started a new family, so it was nice for Adrian and Leah to visit often. Arguments would flare up from time to time but I can say wholeheartedly that we raised those children together. A blended family at its best and worst.

It was like I had picked up from where I left off before I got married. With a thriving jewelry business and a partner that loved and adored me—or so I thought—life was perfect. I was healthy, happy, and filled with confidence.

It's incredible how denial works. There were rumors and whispers that Jeremy was unfaithful but I did not believe it for one second. He loved and adored me and only me. He didn't believe in marriage and after all, he was still young. Those are just a few things I told myself to cover up what my gut was trying to tell me. Quite often I would wake up in the middle of the night crying in agony. I would have this recurring dream, that would change slightly but it was the same dream over and over again. Jeremy would be walking away from me, he would barely look back as he said, "I'm leaving you." But that was not enough to get through to me. My spiritual practice had gone dormant to a certain extent. I would still talk to God, but I wasn't doing much listening.

After about four years together, Jeremy decided to go back to school since he hadn't finished university. With family living in the UK, he decided to go finish his studies there. I was devastated but in full support, of course. I loved him so much. I was all for his betterment. As the time drew nearer for him to leave, it became more and more difficult, to the point where I couldn't get my head around what was about to happen. I considered breaking up but I could not bear the thought. Jeremy filled me like no man ever had. He was loving and compassionate. He was demonstrative and always made me feel like the most beautiful, sexiest woman in the room *and* we never really argued. I was determined to make it work at any cost. I confided in my acupuncturist and homeopathic doctor who occasionally counseled me on personal matters. His advice...? He told me to go with him, help him find an apartment, help him decorate it, then plan my visits in advance, putting a time limit on our time apart. This, he said, would help ease that anxiety and so we did it.

We flew to London, found the perfect place and before you knew it he was settled in. I returned to Jamaica with a heavy heart but a plan. I was going back in just seven weeks. We would text constantly, I would go there, he would come to Jamaica and it felt like it was working just fine.

While using his computer one day, I went to log into my email but his account was up. Afraid of what I would find, I quickly tried to log out when I noticed an email from Michelle. Who the hell is Michelle? I asked myself. I couldn't resist and opened the email. I realized it was a familiar and intimate exchange and my body went weak. I barely made it to the bathroom before I threw up uncontrollably. I had to go back and read it again. Maybe I misunderstood something, possibly even overreacted. Nope, it was the same words, with the same meaning. I went to the bedroom, packed my bag and was ready to leave him but then I went back to the bedroom and unpacked my bag, convincing myself that I must have gotten it all wrong. This was impossible, I thought. Maria's voice was constantly whispering in the back of my mind, this was yet another confirmation of what she was trying to tell me from the start. He came home and I asked him to sit as I had to ask him something. Before I knew what hit me, he had convinced me that I was confused, emotional, and had made up a story in my head. Michelle was just a classmate that loved to mess around.

"Baby, I love you and only you," he professed.

I had cried so much leading up to his arrival that I was spent and fell asleep shortly after our confrontation. We never spoke about it again. There were other occasions where I suspected infidelity. I would go into my jealous rages every so often but he had the key to making me calm down and turning it all into a figment of my imagination. All along, the dreams continued. I would even tell him about the dreams as I would wake up bawling from time to time with him right beside me. "Babe, I can't believe you are still having those awful dreams." he would say.

Jeremy graduated and returned to Jamaica after two and a half years and, naturally, we moved in together. At least I thought it was natural. He had just started a business, and through his interest in polo, tennis, badminton, and cricket, the extracurricular sports favored by Jamaica's well-to-dos, our relationship became exposed to a wider circle. He was given some sort of validation. He came from a very good family but dating me changed things a bit for him. Suddenly, I was no longer dating a "young boy," Jeremy was now Sandra's partner. Everyone knew us as a committed couple that chose not to marry. We were a family. Adrian was now ten and Leah nine. He was their stepdad and they genuinely loved and respected one another and that made me so very happy. The peace and calm my heart felt having the three people I loved the most under the same roof was euphoric.

Jeremy called me our "relationship manager." Every time we were faced with logistical issues or if I wanted to simply implement "relationship improvement" techniques, I'd have it covered. *Men are From Mars, Women are from Venus,* by John Gray—this became my bible.

Life was nice; really, really nice. I had it all. My business was doing extremely well. I had established my jewelry business selling unique, high-end collections at a prestigious boutique in Kingston, Jamaica in 1997 and by 2000, I had an exclusive clientele and an impeccable reputation, and by 2004, both my clientele and inventory had grown into a diverse and lucrative business that I was very proud of. I took my business very seriously, as it meant everything to me. It was my dream come true, after all. I had a brand of my own. If it came in a white gift bag with white tissue paper and out of a white box... it was a piece from Sandra. Frequently commissioned to create custom made pieces for special occasions or for tastemakers simply wanting to make a statement, I became the go-to source for quality jewelry, thoughtfully made with love and integrity. Discretion was also an asset and a must. As it became apparent from very early on, people were very interested in other people's business on this island paradise. They call it "small town mentality." I just figured people had nothing else to do.

Jeremy did not believe in marriage so neither did I. I couldn't disagree because then it would mean he just didn't want to marry *me*, so I went along with it. It's just a piece of paper, I would repeat. I wanted that piece of paper and no matter how hard I tried to convince the world that it made no difference, the truth became more apparent. But I adored him and the life "we lived" and he loved me and the life "we lived." He provided a sweet spot of desire for me and I him. Being in a relationship with me must have been quite comfortable. After the wife bootcamp I was initiated into, I wore my homemaker hat well. My household staff were well trained and ran a tight ship. The refrigerator was always well stocked with all types of goodies for my guests. My house was a pit stop. On any given day, my house would become either a ladies' gathering or an afternoon lime. The kids often had friends over after school. Sometimes just for the fun of it, other times to study for exams. The dining table was often covered in cartridge paper as there was always some class project being constructed.

A Cuban cafecito was usually on the menu when the moms came to pick up—except on Wednesdays, when we would have the regional power outages and Adrian and Leah's cousins would come over and the seven of them would play "murder in the dark" in their basement playroom. Third World Problems.

Fine, you don't want to sign a paper, then at least give me a diamond ring. Demonstrate to the world that you love and respect me, I would say. I laugh as I write, recalling how silly I was. I actually believed my own BS. They say, "Ignorance is bliss" and I can attest to that. Sweet, delicious, and delightful bliss... until that one night. I was in the shower and Jeremy was brushing his teeth.

"My flight leaves at 8 a.m. so I'll need to be at the airport by 6 a.m.," I reminded him through the shower curtain.

It was like he didn't even hear me as I wrapped the towel around me.

He turned to me and said, "I'm moving out."

I asked him to repeat himself. "Pardon?"

"I'm moving out," he said once again.

I could not believe my ears. What was I hearing? Yes, it was obvious that we were going through a rough patch. After practically ten years, a rough patch was expected. I was prepared, we would work through it. I never in my life imagined my life without Jeremy. *ever.* But like I said before and I will continue to say, what is meant to be will be. I left my marriage exactly when I did to spare my children from experiencing a divorce when they were older and better able to understand but I couldn't protect them from the experience after all. It was their lot in life and they were going to suffer it one way or the other. That was the first thought that went through my head. Then it was fear, paralyzing anguish. Now remember, I was to catch a flight in the morning. Oh yeah... I was off on a badass girls' weekend with my new, fun, "facety," fashion-diva girlfriend Alba.

I cried, I begged, I pleaded, I even tried to negotiate. What was I going to do to make him stay? What piece of me was I willing to hand over to be sacrificed? Then suddenly a sense of calm took over my body.

"You are leaving? Cool. I will call Jr. and ask him to please carry me to the airport in the morning. I'm not sure when I will be returning but when I do I want every single sign of you to be out. Everything!"

The children were going to stay home and in his care for the extent of my trip.

"Their father will keep them." I jabbed.

Alba had already checked in and was excitingly jumping up and down while she waved.

"Party time!"

She got a look in my eyes and her mood instantly shifted from glee to utmost concern.

"What is wrong?"

I believe I was running on adrenaline and gradually falling into a catatonic state. I made it onto the plane, I buckled my seatbelt, and as I sat there waiting for takeoff, looked down on my boarding pass and noticed the date. It was Jan 11. 111. That was and will always be my number. Everyone knew it. My friends would constantly send me messages or images with the numbers 111. That number had been showing up for me for as long as I can remember. 111 Rue Rivoli, Paris was a very important place for me, Angie lived in Apt. 111, and countless other instances came up with the numbers 111. I knew what it meant and I lived by its guidance. If 111 shows up for me, I stop, even just mentally, do a full body and mind scan then ask, "Why are you here?" Of course, you're showing up. I'm observing!! I'm paying attention to you as I look up toward God. I live as awakened as I possibly can. I stay in that state as best as I can naturally and other times I have to just nudge, "Pssst, look up." But I could barely stand up straight, much less look up. I was destroyed. Alba did her best to handle me with kid gloves but all I could do was ponder. How am I going to survive this? What will become of me and the kids? What will I say to people? The shame, the humiliation, the truth!

After about two days on South Beach, I instinctively dialed my best friend Stacy and told her I was coming the next day. She did not ask me a single question.

"We should be home; if not, your key will be downstairs," she said.

I flew into JFK in the middle of the day. "3rd between 18 and 19th please," I replied to the taxi driver when he asked, "Where to?"

I walked into the lobby. Will turned towards the key closet as he noticed me arrive, and made his way to help me with my luggage.

"Happy to see you again, Sandy. Stacy went to pick up the kids from school," he gestured with his warm and welcoming smile.

I went upstairs, curled up on the gigantic white sofa, and fell right to sleep. I heard voices and the lighting changed. It went from sunlight to lamplight, then no light. I only noticed in those brief moments when I split my eyelids. I must have slept for about 24 hours straight before Stacy rested a cup of tea on the large white leather ottoman and then I drifted off to sleep once again. I'm sure the scene from *Sex and the City* after "Big" leaves Carrie at the altar comes to mind. Well, add total desolation, take away the makeup and mix in a real life crumbling, and you'll see me.

I started this story with a scene where I said I never thought that I would have to suffer such pain again. Well, this was the first time I had ever felt so devastated. No exaggeration. It was horrid. He had left me and I had to come to terms with it. I had to come out of hiding and tell my nearest and dearest before they found out. Some people found out, others simply figured it out. He had been out publically with "her." I've heard it said, "It's the wife that finds out last." I wasn't his wife but just weeks earlier, Jeremy had upgraded my diamond ring, bought me a new car, and we were buying a house. The architect had even already delivered the remodeling plans, so you can say we were "like" a married couple.

I put myself together the best I could and returned home. I picked up the children from their dad's that night, and before they could rush up to their rooms, I asked them to meet me in the living room.

"I need to talk to you guys." They both ran and flopped their bodies onto the sofa.

"Yeah?" they asked excitedly, expecting some cool news.

I did not know how to put the words together but I had to figure something out. I could not wait for them to notice Jeremy's absence without an explanation.

"What is it, Mummy?" they asked again.

The nerves had me fidgeting with my hands, when Adrian exclaimed, "You're getting married!?" with a bright smile on his face.

I didn't realize I had been playing with the ring Jeremy had just given me to appease my subtle hints, in efforts to remain calm and avoid breaking down in front of them.

"Oh!? No," I said as I realized what I had been doing and quickly folded my hands. "No, Uncle Jeremy and I decided to live separately. We are no longer happy together, so he has moved out. We both love you very much. This has absolutely nothing to do with you guys."

That was pretty much the same exact speech David and I gave them when he and I separated and although they were ten years older now, Adrian 14 and Leah 13, their expressions were so very similar. In utter confusion, they responded simultaneously. "What?" I did my best to explain and then it was time for bed. Adrian called it, "I'm sleeping with Mummy!" and right there the transfer of power took place. Adrian was suddenly back in his rightful place: the man of the house.

Getting over Jeremy took quite some time, lots and lots of tears, and a lot of work. Eckhart Tolle was a spiritual leader I followed closely. His book, *A New Earth*, was just released at the time and I immersed myself in it. I bought the book, the audiobook, and joined the rest of his fans on Oprah's first live webinar. Talk about timing. I made the Now, stillness, and the awareness of my thoughts my focus. I removed myself from the situation and the thoughts around it. Like Eckhart says, "The past has no power over the present moment." Then, practically a year after Jeremy had left and I was feeling close to normal, whatever that means, I was made aware of some shocking information. Jeremy had been cheating on me with a girl that was in our circle of friends. For two years! Talk about sending me back down the rabbit hole of pain and disillusion. But with the support of good friends, God, and my manifestations I was able to recover from that blow. Out at a party one day, I saw her and all I could feel was compassion. She was a woman just like me, made of skin and bones just like me. She also had a heart, just like me. I walked over to her, extended my hands, and asked her if I could speak with her for a moment. With fear in her eyes, she took my hands as I led her to a bench where we sat. "Did he hurt you?" I asked. Tears began to pour out of her eyes as she nodded her head, "Yes." I asked her if he promised to leave me for her.

She whimpered, "All the time."

I put my arm around her and said, "I am so sorry." She too was suffering. He had left us both.

She looked at me, a bit confused and said, "No, I am sorry, Sandra. I am so, so sorry."

Looking right into her eyes, I told her I forgave her and we made a vow. We would not shed one more tear over him. We would take back our power.

"The past has no power over the present moment," I said to her.

She agreed and that's exactly where we left it.

My first experience with true forgiveness was an emotion that lingered for days after. Like you would feel after a really scary ride or a really good movie that stays with you for days, it was like a rush—pure elation. I did that and I am grateful to God for giving me the capacity to love another soul that way. And to set the record straight, I do not hate Jeremy, in fact, it didn't take long to forgive him. He did his best, as we all do. He was so young when we got together. He spent ten years of his life being that man I wanted, caring for me and the kids how I wanted, and we had so much fun. I thank him and know that he had no choice but to go. The pain was mine to overcome and it had nothing to do with him. It was my ego that was crushing me. My identity, how I was viewed, and the fear of the unknown is what had me paralyzed. I was dependent on him to be whole. I lived like that for some time. Who was going to validate me as a good woman, worthy of love and admiration? No one, not the married one, the workaholic, not the narcissist, no one. The only one that could heal my wounds and validate me as a woman was myself. That is something that took a lot of work and a huge amount of introspection.

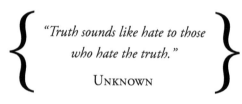

*"Truth sounds like hate to those who hate the truth."*

Unknown

# CHAPTER SIX
# GOD AND ME

**God was a part of my life for as long as I could remember. It was part of my culture and... He came to me himself. I was NEVER alone. Every step I made, God was with me. There had to be more to it—I was sure of that—and I was going to learn all about it.**

S
ome children have imaginary friends; I had God. I thought I was talking to myself but as the years passed and life began to unfold, the answers to my questions would, too.

I was the baby, the smallest, the cutest—and everyone in the family adored me. It was 1971 when my uncle arrived from Cuba with his wife, Tia Elentia. She was amazing—beautiful, full of life, and full of confidence. She had long dark hair and always had her nails done with red nail polish. She smoked cigarettes and when she flashed her ashes into the ashtray, her gold bracelet full of charms would jingle like musical notes. Each charm represented something significant to her. I couldn't take my eyes off of her—or her bracelet, for that matter. That's when I first fell in love with jewelry and the sentiment it can carry.

The best part of it all was that she loved me. We were inseparable. "Perico, voy contigo," she would say. "Little bird, I'm coming with you." I was petite, so my other nickname was "piojo." Yes, that's Spanish for "louse". Terms of endearment for Cubans didn't really sound as such, but any attention I got was good for me. Tia's long, dark, wavy hair, her smell, the way she did her makeup—I couldn't get enough of her. Also, she was pregnant and the whole family was thrilled, even me. The excitement was palpable. A baby!

When Betty was born, it was the most magical time for all of us. Gloria, Barbara, Susie, and I would hover over her while Tia changed her diaper.

"Piojo, please bring me a diaper."

I took off down the hall. I was in charge of bringing the diaper. It was *my* job. Little did I know that Gloria, Barbara, and Susie would come racing to beat me to it. It didn't take much to knock me over and the bright red elephant that Tia had on the dresser went tumbling with me to the ground. Tia heard the crash and came rushing to see what happened. When she realized that the elephant was broken she picked up what she could and smashed the pieces even more against the floor. I looked on with terror. In that very instant, everything changed for me forever. I was no longer her favorite. I broke her elephant therefore my standing, in her eyes, changed. I was convinced that because of this and the fact that baby Betty required so much of her time, I was no longer her "favorite."

Many years later, at a workshop I attended, I was asked to complete an exercise and come back the next day to discuss it. The exercise was to consider this: "When did everything that you knew to be true change for you? What happened and what did you make it mean?" Right there, clear as day, after so many years of feeling like I was no longer special, like I no longer held the "est" space—I say "est" because I never felt like the prettiest, the sexiest, the smartest, the one—I knew it was because of that day, the day Tia smashed the elephant, that changed everything for me. As I grew older, I found myself feeling quite lonely. I felt like I stood out like a sore thumb. I suppose the mere fact that I was relentlessly teased by most of my family members didn't help either. Being the young*est* was no longer a bonus. As my cousins and sister began to blossom, I still had braces, a bad haircut, and I was as skinny as a rail. Like my mom would sometimes joke, I was all teeth.

Let's talk about my mom for a moment. Amelia Amparo Peraza, a Capricorn: quick witted, a sense of humor that can make anyone double over in laughter, and common sense that could not be matched. If Nena—that is her nickname—said it, it was a fact. No need to double-check it, it doesn't matter the topic. She was also the first to arrive in the US out of her entire family. Interestingly enough, when my parents decided to leave Cuba, my dad left first, then two years later and with a marriage by proxy in between, my mom joined him in NYC. I guess that's why she never had a wedding ring. I always wondered how she felt seeing all her sisters-in-law with their symbols of love and commitment displayed for everyone to see. Years later, for their 50th wedding anniversary, I helped my dad select a magnificent white gold eternity diamond band and the diamond engagement ring he couldn't give her then.

In those days, when leaving Cuba, you had to go through another country first. Believe it or not, my mom's country was Jamaica. She spent 28 (worst in her life) days in Kingston, in 1961, just a year before Jamaica's independence.

The Spanish word Nena translates to baby and was a fitting nickname as my mother was the youngest of ten—seven brothers and two sisters—who all spoiled her. Imagine, the baby of the family, at age 25, leaving everything she knew to join her husband that she hadn't seen for two years in some strange land. No Skype, no texting, no social media. Nothing. He was her one and only love—and remember, they weren't even married yet when he left. Once she got to my dad, she began to overcome the culture shock and the language barrier quite quickly. Our home became the migration hub of the family, mostly from my mom's side. They were anti-Castro and although my dad's side were Fidelistas, my dad didn't want anything to do with any of it, so he and my mom didn't really clash heads when it came to politics. My warrior instincts came straight from my mom.

My dad worked hard. He was the superintendent of the building we grew up in and my mom was his right hand, the caretakers of all family members arriving from the homeland. We lived a modest life but in my eyes, we were rich. The building we lived in was absolutely beautiful, the Art Deco design Terrazzo floors with copper inlay, were always polished to perfection. The waitlist was long and people paid big bucks to get on it. The reality of it was, when people left the building, it was usually straight to heaven. No one moved out. Its location was prime, and if I do say so myself, it was impeccably kept. Susie and I were the super's daughters so we were pretty much royalty, or so we thought. It's amazing the stories we can tell ourselves as kids and as adults.

My parents put us through private Catholic school and we were sent to church every Sunday—they didn't go but we had no choice. We didn't mind, though, as any chance to see our friends outside of school was always welcomed.

Although my parents didn't engage in the public worship of God, it was definitely an important part of our growing up and I loved it. Being far from other Cubans or anything remotely similar, we lived a bit differently from the typical Cubans. No plastic on the furniture, no saints with candles at their feet, nor did we have Jesus Christ's picture in every room. My mom had a small figurine of St. Jude, my dad, an abstract version of the Virgin Mary and Lent was observed and celebrated in our home—that was about it.

A little about my dad now. A Scorpio. He was a very serious man. Always well dressed, he would wear nice slacks with either a mock-neck pullover or a crisp polo-style shirt and he was proud of his two perfect girls. My dad instilled strong family values in us, insisting that we only spoke Spanish at home, never used foul language, dressed appropriately, were polite and exhibited good manners at all times. He always said, "Never go back in life, always do better." Oh and no makeup, no nail polish, and *no* boys, ever. I idolized my dad but respected (feared) him as well. When he walked through the door, I would check myself to be sure all was in order. No feet on the furniture, no slackness on the TV, and definitely no eating anywhere else but the kitchen. Helloooooo.

I didn't have a close relationship with my dad. In my mind, Susie was the favorite. The first born—it took my mom five years to get pregnant with her and Susie almost died when she was born. So I get it, I do, but back then I didn't. Again, I didn't feel like I was the "est" in my dad's eyes, either. It wasn't until I was a lot older, when my kids were born and he had fallen sick, that our relationship began to flourish. Thankfully, we had our occasional conversations where he apologized for not being the "dad I deserved," is how he put it, and we became quite close up until the day he passed in 2012.

I watched a lot of TV growing up. PBS in particular. That's where they ran Sesame Street, Mr. Rogers' Neighborhood, and the latest in spiritual programming. One day, as I sat in the new recliner and relaxed in front of the TV, a voice from whatever program was on began to lead what must have been a meditation class.

"Close your eyes, and relax your body," I thought, sure, I can do this.

I was already aware that I was a bit different, a very emotional and deep-feeling individual with all the traits of an empath. I couldn't have been older than nine years old. I followed the instructions, and it was like time stood still. No one was home, which was also odd. Before I knew it, I was in a deep meditative state. Suddenly I felt a presence and a warm yellow light just in front of me. Yes, I peeked, of course I did —I needed to know what it was. All I saw through the slits of my eyes was the yellow light glowing before me.

"I am always with you," I heard another voice say.

I did not flinch. I was calm and feeling so grateful for that moment, even though I don't think I fully understood what it meant then. When it was over, I allowed myself to come out of this "meditation" and went on my merry way. I never doubted that experience to be anything else but the truth. God came to me to let me know he was going to use me. As if I was being appointed in a way.

I am filled with gratitude for how I was raised and I hope to have passed on at least some of what my parents gave me to my children.

One day, not too long ago, during a family gathering, I reminded Tia about the elephant and revealed to her how that situation made me feel. Tears came to her eyes while she explained what actually took place that day.

"I had to smash that elephant that day. For Cubans or anyone who follows spiritual superstition, putting an elephant with its trunk facing the door is a way to protect the home from bad energies. If the elephant breaks it must be broken completely as to break away any negative energy the elephant has absorbed. I couldn't explain that to you, you were only four years old. You were too young to understand."

Something as simple as that influenced every relationship I had since, but if my faith and friendship in God had not been such powerful things, it might have turned out very differently for me.

*"Life is awareness, awareness is life. The degree of your awareness is the degree of your loving. The greater your awareness the greater your loving. The more you open to Spirit, the more clearly you see and the more completely you love. When you become one with Spirit, there is no separation from anything or anyone. There is only loving of the one thing-your divine self, the God this is you and that is also everyone and every thing else."*

JOHN ROGER

# CHAPTER SEVEN
# JACK

**He was tall and handsome and he loved me. To this day, the connection to Jack remains. People come into your life for "a reason, a season, or a lifetime"—Jack was all three.**

---

Back from Florida, where I spent the holidays with my family, I sit here in Malibu, Soho House, with my other family. I call Stacy, Keith, Olivia, and Julian my other family because we have been through it all together. Stacy was a gift from another ex. Jack and I dated briefly in NY. That was what you would call a whirlwind affair.

The year was 1990 when I returned from Paris an established model, represented by some of the best agencies around the world. I lived on the 25th floor of Gerard Towers in Queens. My view: the NYC skyline. I was just 23 years old at the time but after living on my own in Paris, it was difficult to go back home. I had an offer to sublease this apartment and I took it. Thinking back now, I know this was difficult for my family, but it was just the way life happened for me. Life would present me with options, opportunities, choices—and I try to make the most of them. It's almost like a riddle I must solve.

I had lived in that apartment for about a year when I met Jack. Although we didn't really date very long, it was quite an interesting relationship. We met at Indochine, the who's who haven of the fashion industry in those days. He walked in and sat at a table near mine. After a few minutes, he approached my table and asked if he could join me. I was with friends but the seat in front of me was empty. I allowed him to sit down and we proceeded to make conversation. He asked what my plans were for the night. I told him we were going to the bar next door and invited him to join us afterwards. We left separately but he had taken me up on my invitation. Jack walked into the crowded bar and made his way all the way to the back where I was standing. I really couldn't believe he actually came. He invited me to his apartment so we could talk. It was the early 1990s and the world was still somewhat a safe place. I turned to my friend Patty and asked her what she thought. She gave him a once over and then gave me the go ahead.

"Have fun," she said.

We walked over to his place in the West Village. His place was pristine, and furnished impeccably with unique Art Deco pieces. I sat in one chair and he sat in the other, and we began to talk.

"Tell me about your mom," I asked.

"My mom has cancer. She's dying."

It was the saddest thing I had ever heard.

"She doesn't have much time left," he said.

We talked about a few other things, smiled a lot, then he said: "It's getting late, I will do the gentlemanly thing and put you in a taxi home."

We took the elevator and as we made our way down, he kissed me gently on my lips. I got into a cab and smiled all the way home.

The next morning, he called.

"What is your address?" he asked.

"I live in Queens," I responded.

"I know you do—you told me last night. What is your address? I want to come see you."

I gave him the address and he came out to see me.

Jack was smitten with me and I with him. We just could not wipe the smiles from our faces. I was heading to Los Angeles for a shoot but he begged me not to go.

"I'm going up to see my mom tomorrow and would like for you to join me."

It was so strange how incredibly familiar we became in such short time. Jack and I became instantly consumed by one another and nothing else mattered. I know, I've said that before, but that's how I felt each time. When I called the agency to let them know I was cancelling the job they were furious. That was not like me at all, but I liked him a lot and he liked me. I would stay at his apartment pretty often and from time to time his ex-girlfriend, Stacy, would call.

"Hi, can I speak with Jack please?" She was always so nice that her calls never made me feel jealous.

Once his mom passed, so did the romance. Yes, I think it's interesting as well. I was there for him in the way he needed at such a painful time. That's when I decided to move to Miami. It was perfect timing. I was heartbroken and needed a change of scenery so I picked up my belongings and headed south. Miami had a special energy to it. The old hotels were being refurbished and reopened one after the other, and the streets of South Beach had been cleaned of the drug-infested element they were harboring.

Although my relationship with Jack really didn't go anywhere, he has never left me. At different occasions through the 26 years since, someone connected to Jack has crossed my path in one way or another.

I settled into my new apartment on Miami Beach and the first thing I did was head to A Fish Called Avalon, a new restaurant owned by friends of mine who had also relocated from New York City.

"A martini please, but in my martini glass please."

Up on the shelf was my special martini glass. It was a little bigger than the rest and was for me alone.

The bartender walked over to the shelf, carefully lifted my glass, and turned to me and asked, "This one?"

I was taken aback for a moment. It was Stacy, Jack's ex-girlfriend. She had started working there days before I moved. She smiled and made me my martini.

Jack and Frankie, his best friend at the time, had flown into town. Jack had come looking for me. I have no idea how he found me—this was a time before cellular phones—but where there's a will, there's a way, I guess. Jack and I were walking back to my apartment when Stacy turned the corner with her friend, Laura. What are the chances I thought, not only does she work where I frequent but she lives close by as well? They too had recently moved to Miami and were living just a few blocks away from me. We stopped to say hello, then went on our merry way.

Jack and I tried to make it work. He came to visit a few times but that quickly fizzled.

A few weeks later, at the local pool hall, a guy approached me.

"Do I know you?" he asked.

He looked familiar but I couldn't recall from where. We both thought about it a bit, as it was gnawing at us.

"Yes," he said excitedly. "Do you ever go to Indochine?"

"In New York?" I asked.

"Yes, I was sitting in the booth."

I was shocked. When we had initially walked into the restaurant there was a group waiting to be seated as well and they sat at the table across from us. Our eyes had locked but I guess my attention was totally distracted when Jack walked in. It felt a little surreal. How does something like that happen? We chuckled, shook our heads, and proceeded to introduce ourselves.

"My name is George and this is Neil," he said.

Shortly after, George introduced me to his friends Nicolas, Blaise, and Mo.—the Jamaican crew I spoke about before, a really nice group of guys. They were all single except Neil; he had just started dating a model from New York.

Stacy and I grew close and formed a friendship of our own. She and I were walking home after she got off work one evening, when she invited me in for a drink. Laura was there with her boyfriend.

"Neil?"

"Sandra?"

We were both speechless.

"This is your girlfriend?"

We all started to laugh in amazement. It was crazy. Months earlier, all the way in New York, we had already been destined to be friends and we did become really tight.

Laura and Neil eventually moved in together, leaving Stacy homeless. We still laugh about it to this day. Stacy lived out of my closet for a few months and whenever she sat on the floor to sort through her mound of belongings we would sing, "...but she's homeless, la da di la di da," from Gypsy Woman by Crystal Waters.

Stacy has been my best friend for the past 26 years and we have all remained friends, including George, whom I went to visit in Brickell the day I manifested the move to Miami, after the break up with Jeremy.

I have a few other examples of the "Jack connections." Like Mike, whom I visited in LA earlier this year. Mike introduced himself via DM on Instagram. We began a flirtatious exchange while I was trying to detach myself from the clutches of my Twin Flame affair. I decided I would go meet him, and since I had other good friends living in LA, I figured if it went badly, I would still be able to have a good time. Yes, I did my due diligence beforehand. I checked out his "followers" and noticed Jack was among the list. That was the green light.

I called Jack and asked, "Is this guy ok? Or is he a creep?"

Jack gave his thumbs up and I booked my flight. We met on Manhattan Beach for lunch and had a lovely time. He seemed so into me and all the while I was thinking that the whole situation was so very interesting.

"Wait here, I'll go get the car."

While I stood there facing the ocean, that feeling, the one I described earlier? It washed over me yet again. I was manifesting. I like it here, I thought, I like it a lot. I had reached a point where Jamaica had gotten way too small and the ceiling too low. No pun intended, although that is how I described "The Dungeon." The apartment felt so small, it was like the ceiling was weighing down on my head.

I returned to Jamaica and never heard from Mike again. It was like he served his purpose. He got me to visit LA so I could somehow come to this realization. Again, LA had come up. When I met Jack I was headed there, when I left New York City I was headed there, when I met David I was headed there. After Jeremy left me and I decided to give my modeling career another go, I was set up on a blind date with Sean, an LA resident but that didn't pan out either. I guess it wasn't time for our connection to stick then. Sean is now married to Stella and they have two of the most gorgeous children, three-year-old Louis and Hendrix who's about to turn one. Actually, Sean is originally from Jamaica, so we have that sense of camaraderie and he has now become one of my dearest friends. Once I made up my mind about moving out to LA, I looked up all my friends and stayed with each of them so that I could get a real feel of the place. It was a huge move, not to mention a major decision, so I wanted to make sure I liked it here.

Still, I miss my friends, and my son (who now works in the family business), and the family I cultivated through the

25 years on the "Rock." I miss the hot sun and the gorgeous hills and valleys. I will always love that island paradise. And who knows... I might just end up back there one day.

When change comes our way, the best thing to do is embrace "what is." Without acceptance, there is resistance. That's not a vibration that gets us anywhere. Let go, ride the wave, and observe. Welcome the lesson and the opportunity to stretch, grow, and elevate as a servant of God. The happier we are, the better our surroundings. The ripple effect of being in a peaceful frequency changes the world and those around us. If we could do that, something as simple as being kind to our neighbor, smiling with the cashier at the supermarket, or just looking someone in the eye when at the bank, we can improve someone's life, someone's vibration, and the response towards his or her day. I want to do that.

In the meantime, that chair—the one for my life partner —remains vacant. If you really don't want to sit there, please move or I'll move you myself. If you really do want to sit there, then by all means—but you can't sit there unless I allow you to.

Yes, I've been through a lot. I've also had a lot of support, from so many good friends and family. I have endured a lot but we know that God doesn't give us more than we can handle. I'm living proof of that.

> *"Life is not merely a series of meaningless*
> *accidents or coincidences, uh uh,*
> *but rather it is a tapestry of acts that*
> *culminate in an exquisite, sublime plan."*

FROM THE FILM SERENDIPITY

CHAPTER EIGHT

# MANIFESTATION

**My life coach calls me "the master manifester." I speak it and it happens. Is it possible to manifest too much?**

---

I have a secret to share. Well it's not really a secret but it's also not something I go around advertising. Once I imagine something, or simply think about it a whole lot to the point that I can feel it in my soul, it happens. I don't mean just ask for something; I'm referring to that moment when you don't even try. I have a thought, it resonates, I visualize it and the visceral acknowledgment occurs. Time and time again, I have manifested things, places, jobs, even boyfriends. I honestly believe that I didn't even know when I was doing it until the "wishes" came true.

It was my friend Rita's 13th birthday and, believe it or not, Susie and I were actually allowed to go to her party. Her parents, although very strict as well, were kinda cool. They mostly stayed in the bedroom while we played our records, danced and, of course, talked about the new boy at school. The girls were crazy about him. He was so cute, tall for a 13-year-old, dark hair, rosy cheeks, and the sweetest, most devilish smile I had ever seen. I was obsessed with John Cubano. He was Susie and Rita's age and I was a year younger, so all I did was listen in as the girls gushed about their crush.

Susie and Rita were so pretty, smart, and popular that everyone was wondering which one of the two he'd end up asking out. Did I mention he was funny too? I liked him so much that I didn't care that he called me Bucky Dent, like the baseball player. Not for his talent but because I had braces. Everyone had a nickname, that's just how John was. Every night, without fail, I would go to sleep repeating, John Cubano, in my head. Everyone who knew me, knew about John.

Well, to make a long story short and get back to the point, I'm pretty sure John was my first manifestation. I knew, for a fact, that he would be my boyfriend. I knew that he would be my first kiss. So said, so done. At age 13, this ugly duckling had the boyfriend of her dreams, and it was a real confidence booster for me at the time.

I tell this part of my story with a heavy heart. John died in a tragic car accident in 2013. After so many years, he had remained very close to our family. The news of his passing came just eight months after the passing of my dad. I have never suffered the loss of anyone like I did John's. It was an uncontrollable and profound pain that I felt for some time. I cried so much for so long, all day and all night, until a feeling of closure came over me – like a part of my youth was crossing over with him. I feel him all the time and when I'm feeling down, or just out of sorts, John's son reaches out, as if to remind me that he's right there with me.

We were expecting Dad's passing, but it almost felt like it would never happen. He survived so much longer than the doctors expected. Bonus years, we called them. As a family, we chose quality over quantity. So between the cocktail of natural supplements and his pharmaceutical potion, we were able to avoid chemotherapy and its debilitating side effects. The days leading up to his death were pretty surreal. My whole being went into automatic pilot. Each family member took their role and we started making arrangements. It was so incredibly interesting and if you are filled with love the way Susie and I were, then it can be one of the most healing times of your life. It becomes a dance... a flow. We took care of each other and the things we knew the other couldn't handle. Just us two. Like my mom always told us growing up, "Now remember, you two are all you have. Take care of each other always."

Ask, and you shall receive. I mean, come on, these sayings don't just come from nowhere. About two years after Jeremy left, things began to change for me again. First Adrian went off to boarding school, then Leah followed a year later. My dad was diagnosed with cancer, the kids were away, and I had given 19 years to Jamaica. This meant no pension or retirement as I had not worked in the US for all those years. It was time to make the move. But how, and what was I going to do? At the same time, I was seeing Robert and although I loved him very much, I had to go. Even he eventually admitted that it was the right thing to do.

I reconnected with one of my friends from my days in Miami. George was part of the design team for one of the new towers in Brickell. It was 2009, and Miami was still rattled by the economic shock of 2008, so there was a lot of real estate inventory, especially on Brickell Ave., and people were buying at very low prices. I went up to George's office and I took in the view while I waited on him to finish up a call. I can remember what the sky looked like and exactly how I felt when I looked out that corner window. It was apt 1109 and the balcony looked over the Biscayne Bay. As I stopped to look at the skyline, I noticed myself saying, "I can do this, I can live here. I can live in Miami," and just like that, the wheels were in motion. I went back to Jamaica convinced that I would make that move... I just had to figure out how.

Days later, a friend introduced me to Peter. Peter was a successful businessman from Montego Bay that wanted to have the interior of his penthouse on Brickell Ave. designed. After getting acquainted, Peter offered me the job, and I was Miami bound. I called my cousin, who is a realtor, and within days he sent a list of four apartments for me to rent. I wasn't able to be in Miami at the time, so I asked him to choose for me. I trusted him and he knew exactly what I needed. When it was time to sign the lease, I flew up to Miami. I parked on the street and when I walked into the apartment, I walked directly towards the window. I manifested this too. I had leased apt 4109. Same apartment line, different floor... same view. I could not believe my eyes. I made it happen, again. I can give you more examples but then we'll get off course. The most important part of manifesting is believing—knowing it has to feel true to you—or it will not happen.

> *"You have sole ownership of your vision. And the Universe will give you what you want within your vision. What happens with most people is that they muddy their vision with 'reality.' Their vision becomes full of not only what they want but what everybody else thinks about what they want, too. Your work is to clarify and purify your vision so that the vibration that you are offering can then be answered."*

ABRAHAM-HICKS

# CHAPTER NINE

# WAS IT FEAR?

**I had no choice but to leave Jamaica and I had to leave him too—but when I heard that I might lose him, I was riddled with fear. Could I lose the last man that would ever love me? I had to get him back. I was sure that all relationships were hard work and I did not want to be alone.**

---

W as it fear that made me get in touch with Robert again? I was speaking on the phone with a friend, and she was planning a trip up to visit me in Miami.

She paused a minute as to choose her words carefully, then asked: "What are you doing, Sandra? Seriously. You say you love this man, right? Last we spoke, that's what you said, right?"

I said, "Yes."

"So what are you doing? I have not seen him with anyone since you left," she informed me. "It was obvious that he was very hurt by your leaving."

I was taken aback when she said that. I was selfish, 100%. I had to go, 99.9%, for real, logical reasons, and I just left.

"If you are not interested, it's fine, but I saw him out with someone and it looks like it was a date," she said.

I felt like someone had poured a bucket of ice water over me. I could barely breathe. We hung up and I began to pace. I was filled with a nervous fear. He might have been finally moving on but I knew that, given my reaction to the memo, I was not at all over him.

Fear is a very interesting reaction. It causes us to behave in an instinctively protective way, even if we are not really afraid. Most of us just go into our reaction catalogue and pick one and go with it, ego in the driver's seat. Fear is the ego telling you everything you need to hear so you stay in that same place. That's where ego has the most comfort. Like a set of old PJs, the ego wants you to snuggle up in that place. Even if deep in your gut you know something is not good for you, there is sometimes comfort in dysfunction.

He was a good man. Robert loved me and I was not going to lose him. No way. I didn't want to be alone either. He could possibly be the last man that could love me like that again. What was I looking for anyway? He was right there. I could make adjustments and allowances, besides, all relationships are difficult. Once conversations are had with an open heart, we could resolve most issues. The joke was over, and it was time to wave the white flag and go home to Jamaica and Robert. I was sure that I wanted to be with him for the rest of my life. I was certain that I would be happy to grow old and care for him as long as we lived.

What made me believe that things would change? Fear again? Fear of being alone?

We also tend to be ok with situations that feel familiar. Robert reminded me of my dad. There was something so secure about him and his demeanor that said, "Leave me alone"—he was a loner, yet he had let me into his space, so close. At least that's how it felt. When my kids were little, I used to tell them to be mindful of when something feels familiar. Just because it does, doesn't mean it's good or good for you. I've done things in ways that weren't necessarily the right way to do them. I am human and I've made mistakes and they should make their decisions based on their own judgment and not based on how their parents went about their lives. Just don't be afraid like I was.

{ *"I think its important to realize you can miss something but not want it back."* }

PAULO COELHO

# CHAPTER TEN

# THE ART OF REPAIR

**All this can't be for nothing... Why would I live all these lives, reinventing myself over and over again? That is when I realized that I was chosen to serve. To give hope, love, and support to as many as I can reach.**

---

I t's been a lovely Christmas. I can't remember the last time I was able to say that. I stood in the elevator filled with peace and contentment, while my nephews—Justin and Joseph—and my children—Adrian now 23 and Leah 22—huddled around a grocery cart overflowing with presents. We were meeting my sister and her boyfriend, Raul, at my Mom's apartment to exchange presents. I took a breath and thought: I've done a good job. I have tried to raise well-balanced, decent adults, as they are.

I no longer feel the heaviness of guilt or the need to balance my thoughts and actions in order to please anyone or to avoid offending others. I live with love in my heart and I express it every chance I get. Life is beautiful. It really is. Magical, if you pay close attention. I am no saint and far from perfect but I am filled with a love that makes me feel light. And when I forget, I reach for my gold cross and ask God to keep me in the light.

Someone commented the other day: "You've lost weight, haven't you?"

My answer was yes, absolutely. I have not dieted nor do I exercise, but I have lost "the weight." I have gotten rid of anything that makes me feel uncomfortable, unhappy, unfulfilled. I have learned the art of letting go. It is such a lovely feeling. I struggle at times but I no longer have knee jerk reactions. I pay attention to my visceral reaction first, then assess. If I feel like there is too much negativity in a particular situation, I remove myself. It's wonderful because it doesn't change how I feel about anyone; we are all at this dance of life together. We chose it and it chose us for a reason and I'm living through it. I am taking every ounce of happiness, pain, and everything in between and giving thanks. I am filled with faith, and the knowing that I am good enough for everyone. After years and years of not feeling like I was enough for my husband, my children, my lovers, even as a friend at times, now I actually feel at peace. There has been a shift. A combination of forgiveness and unconditional love that I learned from my experience with my twin flame, my work with Helen, and the way I stood for myself by leaving a bad relationship. Forgiveness and love for others, yes, but also for myself?

This chapter of my journey has just begun. As I reflect on all the different choices I've made, I am certain that each and every one has been to get me to this very point in my life. This is what I told a friend when she asked me, "Why do you feel you need to write a book, Sandy?"

I responded without giving the question any thought: "Do you really think that God put all He has in my path for me to just live, then die?" I have to do something with all of this. It is my duty to pass on all I have learned, all the lessons and experiences I have come across all these years. There has to be a reason for it, and I am going to follow the signs and the path that has been selected to be mine and mine only. It can't all be for nothing... why would I have lived all these lives? Reinventing myself over and over again. I have acknowledged that I was chosen to serve, to give hope, love, and support to as many as I can reach.

Besides, I think it's a pretty interesting story.

> *"A child is born on that day and at that hour when the celestial rays are in the mathematical harmony with his individual karma."*
>
> SRI YUKTESWAR

# ACKNOWLEDGMENTS

I've been wanting to write a memoir for the past 25 years and the one thing that kept me from actually putting pen to paper was that I didn't have an ending. "Nothing before its time," they say. I didn't have an ending but I did have a beginning—the beginning of this journey. Then Jordane came into my life and the stories began to flow. His inquisitive yet respectful manner got me talking and expressing myself, making me realize that I had something valid to share. Thank you, Jordane, from the bottom of my heart. Then Angela and her team from The Author Incubator appeared like angels in the dark and helped me make my dream a reality. Thank you for considering me, then allowing me to join your outstanding group of authors. I want to also include Tracy Matalon and Sky Jarrett for giving me such great advice and input when I first started the process of joining this marvelous program and Peter Melhado, Tami Chynn, Jodi Gusek and Sean Knibb for brainstorming with me on the final title.

To everyone who worked around my time, constantly soothing my angst about deadlines and reassuring me of my ability to do this in the first place, I am extremely grateful. I want to express profound gratitude to my son, Adrian, who constantly checked on me throughout the entire process, rooting for me from beginning to end and to my daughter, Leah, who was my very own personal line editor, who read over my work and gave me her honest and insightful advice. Also, special thanks to my sister, Susie, and Mom, "Nena," for their endless, loving support and to Tammy Hart for giving me my occasional pep talks, reminding me to write from my heart. Thank you to all my dear friends for just being there each time I needed an ear to bounce ideas off of or a shoulder to cry on when some tough memories surfaced. I would be remiss if I didn't thank my boss, Ard, for being so patient and accepting of my decision to embark on this process while still part of his team and giving me constant support. This "journey back to me" could not have begun without all of you who literally held me during the painful experiences that brought me to this surreal and wonderful place in my life.

To the Morgan James Publishing team: Special thanks to David Hancock, CEO & Founder for believing in me and my message. To my Author Relations Manager, Bonnie Rauch, thanks for making the process seamless and easy. Many more thanks to everyone else, but especially Jim Howard, Bethany Marshall, and Nickcole Watkins.

# THANK YOU

Thank you for reading my book. Join me for a free class on how to make yourself the hero of your own story.

Email me at sandra@cutsofadiamond.com or comment on Facebook at:

https://www.facebook.com/Cuts-of-a-Diamond
-189679371759042/

**Instagram:** sandra_rodriguez_bicknell

**Website:** https://www.cutsofadiamond.com

# ABOUT THE
# AUTHOR

A woman and spiritual being whose focus in life is love, Sandra Rodriguez-Bicknell was born on April 15, 1967 to Cuban immigrants living and working in NYC. Even though she was not born there, her Cuban pride is unmistakable. In 1988, a serendipitous encounter launched her modeling career and transformed her life as she knew it. Before long, Sandra was traveling the world as a top international model. Four years later, at the age of 25, she married the man she called her hero and moved to his homeland, Jamaica, to start a family with him. The marriage ended after six years and two children when Sandra was left to pick up the pieces and reinvent herself, both for her own wellbeing as well as for her children. She fell in love again, but after a blissful ten-year romance, Sandra was once again on her own. It was then that she decided to move back to the states to be near her family and ailing father, who passed three years after. She eventually found herself back in Jamaica rekindling a romance that she had left behind, but this, also, was not meant to be.

Now, as cultured as she is worldly, Sandra has decided to use her experiences to comfort and guide those who are experiencing the same darkness that she herself has endured. The reason she chooses to inspire others through jewelry in the first place is clear: She grew up surrounded by jewelry. Her uncle, who sold one-of-a-kind handmade treasures out of a briefcase, had her mesmerized by beautiful gems from an early age. In the evenings, her aunt would string pearls with a graceful technique under a bright light while a young Sandra watched in fascination. It was there that her love of fine, custom-made jewelry started to develop.

Sandra is now living in California, fulfilling a lifelong dream to work with her clients to create pieces that "mark a moment in time" and helping to inspire others to embrace the power of lifelong self-discovery.

CPSIA information can be obtained
at www.ICGtesting.com
Printed in the USA
FFHW021106240119
50287393-55315FF